$ THE $5 TAKEOUT COOKBOOK

200 Delicious Recipes for Pizza, Chinese, Mexican, and Thai

*Good, Cheap Food
for When You
Want to Eat In*

Rhonda Lauret Parkinson, Margaret Kaeter,
Belinda Hulin, & Jennifer Malott Kotylo

A adamsmedia
Avon, Massachusetts

Contains material adapted and abridged from *The Everything® Pizza Cookbook* by Belinda
Hulin, copyright © 2007 by F+W Media, Inc., ISBN 10: 1-59869-259-3, ISBN 13: 978-1-
59869-259-4; *The Everything® Chinese Cookbook* by Rhonda Lauret Parkinson, Bethany
Brown, and Julie Gutin, copyright © 2003 by F+W Media, Inc., ISBN 10: 1-58062-954-7,
ISBN 13: 978-1-58062-954-6; *The Everything® Mexican Cookbook* by Margaret Kaeter,
copyright © 2003 by F+W Media, Inc., ISBN 10: 1-58062-967-9, ISBN 13: 978-1-58062-
967-6; and *The Everything® Thai Cookbook* by and Jennifer Malott Kotylo, copyright ©
2002 by F+W Media, Inc., ISBN 10: 1-58062-733-1, ISBN 13: 978-1-58062-733-7.

Published by
Adams Media, a division of F+W Media, Inc.
57 Littlefield Street, Avon, MA 02322. U.S.A.
www.adamsmedia.com

ISBN 10: 1-4405-2587-0
ISBN 13: 978-1-4405-2587-2
eISBN 10: 1-4405-2601-X
eISBN 13: 978-1-4405-2601-5

Printed in the United States of America.

10   9   8   7   6   5   4   3   2   1

Library of Congress Cataloging-in-Publication Data
is available from the publisher.

This book is available at quantity discounts for bulk purchases.
For information, please call 1-800-289-0963.

CONTENTS

INTRODUCTION

Pad Thai. Deep-crust pizza. Chimichangas. Pork fried rice. Who doesn't love takeout! There's nothing like coming home from a long, busy day, grabbing the menu of your favorite delivery hotspot, and sitting back while waiting for your food to arrive. The only problem? Takeout's not cheap. But *The $5 Takeout Cookbook* is here to help.

Replicating the familiar flavors in your favorite Chinese, Thai, Mexican, and pizza dishes may seem like an impossible task, but the truth is, you don't have be a skilled chef—or need to spend a lot of money— to create great takeout food without even having to pick up the phone. With $5 or less and basic, fresh ingredients, each recipe comes together just like at a restaurant, if not better. Cooking at home couldn't be easier, cheaper, or more delicious!

One of the most frustrating parts of ordering in is the time you spend waiting for your food to actually get to your house. On a busy weekend, you can find yourself sitting around starving for more than an hour! When you make your own food at home, you control your schedule and your food will be ready right as your roommate gets home from school, your spouse walks in from work, or your kids come home from practice. As for the time involved, most of the work lies in preparation—and you can do that in advance. Time spent actually cooking can be mere minutes, especially if you're stir-frying. And once you've cooked a few meals you'll find yourself falling into a routine—cutting vegetables while the meat is marinating, preparing a sauce while waiting for the oil to reach the required temperature for deep-frying—so your food is ready when you are.

What are the pluses of cooking your takeout favorites at home? Besides the obvious advantage to your wallet, the food you cook at home is often healthier than most takeout fare because you control the fat and calorie count. You can also let your creativity come into play, adjusting a recipe to add favorite foods or seasonal local ingredients. Cooking takeout at home also allows you to modify a recipe to suit your tastes. Don't like onions in your fried rice? Just leave them off! Love red peppers, but don't get enough on your pizza? Throw them on there and enjoy! What you eat is up to you.

With *The $5 Takeout Cookbook* you can now make great-tasting versions of all your takeout favorites at home—and for a fraction of the cost. It's so easy and delicious, you'll wonder why you even bothered to call for delivery!

PART ONE
MEXICAN

The Mexican diet is both flavorful and varied. Dine on lush tropical fruits, bean-stuffed chili peppers, spicy tomato sauces, grilled corn, honeyed sweet potatoes, and cocoa-crusted turkey, and you find yourself in the land of the Aztecs.

Best known for its combinations, it's a rare that you'll find a Mexican dish that uses just one or two ingredients. Meats, for example, are marinated then drenched in sauces containing dozens of ingredients. Fish may be broiled or baked but it is always topped with a unique sauce. Even something as simple as a salad of melon balls will have a tart sauce draped over it.

Now those flavorful dishes of tropical fruits, bean-stuffed chili peppers, spicy tomato sauces, grilled corn, and much more are no longer just a takeout option. *The $5 Takeout Cookbook* has simplified the recipes, so you can make these delectable dishes in your very own home. So get your taste buds ready, and have a great time in the kitchen cooking these fabulous Mexican takeout recipes!

CHAPTER 1

PORK AND POULTRY

Pork Roast with Apples

 Serves 3

1 pound pork roast

¼ teaspoon dried oregano

¼ teaspoon dried thyme

¼ teaspoon dried cilantro

½ teaspoon salt

½ teaspoon ground black pepper

1 tablespoon vegetable oil

½ medium-sized yellow onion

2 garlic cloves

1½ medium-sized green apples (such as Granny Smith)

½ cup apple juice

¼ cup dry white wine

½ envelope unflavored gelatin

Serve with Turnip and Mustard Leaf Rolls (see recipe to follow) for a unique combination of flavors.

1. Preheat oven to 350°F.
2. Season the pork roast with the oregano, thyme, coriander, salt, and black pepper.
3. Heat the vegetable oil in a large frying pan. Add the pork roast. Cook on medium heat, turning the pork roast until all sides are browned.
4. Remove the skin from the onion and cut into 1-inch pieces. Remove the skin from the garlic and cut into thin slices. Remove the stem and core from 1 apple and cut into ½-inch slices.
5. Put the pork roast in a large baking dish. Cover with the apple juice and white wine. Sprinkle the apple pieces, onion, and garlic on top. Cover and bake for 1 hour.
6. Remove the peeling, stem, and core from the remaining apple. Place in a food processor or blender and blend until puréed.
7. Boil ½ cup of water. Add the gelatin. Stir in the apple purée. Cool in the refrigerator for 15 minutes.
8. Remove the meat from the oven. Cut into ½-inch pieces and arrange on a platter. Top with the gelatin mixture right before serving.

TURNIP AND MUSTARD LEAF ROLLS

 Serves 3

½ bunch turnip leaves
½ bunch mustard leaves
2 tablespoons butter
⅛ cup fresh epazote leaves

½ teaspoon salt
½ teaspoon ground black pepper

Any combination of leaves works well. If your local store has a small supply of exotic leaves, try spinach and beet leaves.

1. Remove the stems from the turnip and mustard leaves and wash the leaves thoroughly. Pat dry with a paper towel.
2. Remove the stems from the epazote leaves and mince the leaves.
3. Layer 1 turnip leaf then 1 mustard leaf. Add ½ teaspoon of butter in the center of the mustard leaf. Sprinkle with epazote leaves, salt, and black pepper. Roll up the leaves. Repeat with remaining leaves.
4. Place the leaf rolls in a frying pan with a small amount of water. Cover and turn heat on low. Cook for 10 minutes on low heat.

Pork and Potatoes

 Serves 3

💲 Total Cost: $4.80

1 pound pork roast

1½ large white onions

2 garlic cloves

4 assorted whole chili peppers

2 ½ medium-sized potatoes

5 whole cloves

½ cinnamon stick

5 black peppercorns

½ teaspoon whole cumin seeds

1 tablespoon white vinegar

Serve with Pineapple and Coconut Salad (Chapter 2) for a blending of sweet and spicy.

1. Preheat oven to 350°F.
2. Trim the fat from the pork roast. Peel the onions and cut into quarters. Peel and mince the garlic. Remove the stems from the chili peppers and cut in half lengthwise. (Do not remove the seeds.) Peel the potatoes and cut in half.
3. Place the pork in a large baking pan. Cover with the onions, garlic, chili peppers, cloves, cinnamon stick, peppercorns, and cumin. Add just enough water to cover the ingredients. Cover and cook for 1 hour.
4. Stir the mixture. Add the potatoes, cover, and cook for 1 hour or until the potatoes are soft. Ten minutes before serving, remove the spices and add the vinegar. Leave uncovered for the last 10 minutes.

Mushy Potatoes

Have your raw potatoes gone mushy? They're still good if you use them right away. Remove the peels and slice the potatoes thickly. Put them in a soup or stew and no one will know they were past their prime.

Lonches

Serves 3

3 slices bacon

3 large hard rolls

¼ pound Monterey jack
cheese

¾ cup red chili sauce

Substitute meats and cheeses. Add onions or olive slices.

1. Preheat oven to 350°F.
2. Fry the bacon until crisp. Drain off the grease.
3. Thinly slice the cheese. Split the rolls in half horizontally. Fill generously with cheese and top with a bacon strip. Close the rolls to form sandwiches and place on a baking sheet.
4. Put in the oven for 5 to 10 minutes or until the rolls are hot and the cheese is melted.
5. While the rolls are baking, heat the sauce to bubbling.
6. Place each filled roll in a soup bowl and ladle ¼ cup sauce over the top.

Chorizo (Mexican Sausage)

Makes 1 pound

1 pound ground pork

½ tablespoon paprika

½ teaspoon ground black pepper

½ teaspoon dried oregano

½ teaspoon ground cumin

⅛ teaspoon ground coriander seeds

⅓ cup vinegar

½ teaspoon garlic powder

1 tablespoon salt

1 tablespoon cayenne pepper

1. Place all the ingredients in a large mixing bowl. Mix with your hands until all the ingredients are well blended.
2. Place in an airtight container. Refrigerate for at least 2 days.
3. Form into patties for frying.

Pork with Pineapple

 Serves 4

1½-pound pork loin
½ large white onion
½ large red tomato
⅙ cup sliced pimientos
½ tablespoon vegetable oil
1 cup canned pineapple
chunks, with juice

½ cup canned beef stock (or
1 beef bouillon cube dis-
solved in 1 cup water)
⅛ cup dry sherry
¼ teaspoon chili powder
½ teaspoon salt
¼ teaspoon black pepper
1 tablespoon flour

Serve with red rice.

1. Cut the meat into 2-inch chunks. Peel the onion and chop into ¼-inch pieces. Remove the stem from the tomato and chop into ¼-inch pieces. If using fresh pimientos, cut into ¼-inch strips.
2. Heat the vegetable oil in a large frying pan. Add the meat and brown well on all sides. Add the onion and cook for about 5 minutes or until soft.
3. Add the tomato, pimientos, the pineapple with juice, beef stock, sherry, and chili powder to the skillet; stir until well mixed. Bring to a boil, reduce heat to a simmer, and add the salt and pepper.
4. Cover and simmer until the meat is tender, about 1½ hours. Stir occasionally.
5. Just before serving, sprinkle the flour over the simmering sauce and stir in. Cook and stir until the sauce is thickened.

Use Fresh Garlic
Beware of prepared garlic. While preminced garlic looks like a good buy and certainly sounds easier, it releases an oil while stored after chopping. This affects both the taste and consistency in your recipes. Fresh garlic is always best.

Mexican Pork and Beans

 Serves 2

⅛ pound sliced bacon

⅛ pound boneless pork tenderloin

⅛ pound ham

½ large white onion

¾ cup canned diced tomatoes

½ teaspoon chili powder

¼ teaspoon ground cumin

¼ teaspoon dried oregano

1 cup canned pinto beans

¼ cup tequila

Serve as a stew with fresh flour tortillas.

1. Cut the pork and ham into 1-inch cubes. Peel the onion and slice into ¼-inch rounds.
2. Cook the bacon on medium heat in a frying pan until crisp. Reserve the grease in the pan and transfer the bacon to paper towels to drain. When cool, crumble.
3. Brown the pork and ham in the bacon fat. Add the onion. Turn the heat to medium. Cover and cook until soft, about 5 minutes.
4. Add the tomatoes, chili powder, cumin, oregano, and the crumbled bacon, stir well. Add the beans. Bring to a boil. Gradually stir in the tequila.
5. Continue to cook, uncovered, for 1 hour or until the pork is well done and the mixture is the consistency of a rich stew. Stir occasionally.

Dry Soup?

Many Mexican dishes feature bread or tortillas that are soaked in a sauce until the dish resembles more of a casserole or heavy stew than a soup. In Mexico, they refer to these dishes as dry soups. It's not certain where this name came from, but it's an apt description.

Rice with Sautéed Pork

 Serves 4

Total Cost: $2.41

¾ cup dry white rice

½-pound pork loin

1 small-sized yellow onion

1 cup canned pinto beans

1 tablespoon olive oil

⅛ teaspoon garlic powder

1 (6-ounce) can tomato paste

1 teaspoon salt

¼ teaspoon dried oregano

¼ teaspoon ground cumin

¾ teaspoon medium-hot red chili powder

Serve with Tropical Gelatin (see recipe to follow) and fresh flour tortillas.

1. Bring 3 cups of water to boil in a medium-sized pot. Add the rice; boil for 5 minutes. Reduce temperature to medium-low and simmer for 20 minutes. Drain off excess water.
2. Cut the pork into thin slices. Peel the onion and cut into ¼-inch pieces. Rinse and drain the pinto beans.
3. Heat the oil to medium temperature in a large frying pan. Add the pork and cook until browned. Add the onions, garlic powder, salt, oregano, cumin and chili powder; sauté lightly until the onions are soft and clear but not brown. Stir in the tomato paste and 1 cup of water.
4. Turn heat to low. Cover and simmer for 30 minutes.
5. Add the beans and stir lightly. Cover and simmer for 15 minutes longer.
6. Stir in the rice. Cook, uncovered, for 10 minutes.

TROPICAL GELATIN

 Serves 3

½ cup papaya
½ cup guava
½ cup fresh pineapple
6 lady fingers

1 cup water
1½ packages unsweetened gelatin
¼ cup granulated sugar

1. Remove the rinds and cores from the pineapple, papaya, and guava. Cut the fruit into ½-inch pieces. Measure 1 cup of each fruit and mix together in a small mixing bowl. (Do not drain the juice from the fruit.)
2. Break the lady fingers into 1-inch pieces and line the bottom of 3 individual custard bowls with the pieces.
3. Bring the water to boil in a medium-sized pot. Add the gelatin and sugar; stir until both are dissolved. Remove from heat and stir in the fruit.
4. Let cool at room temperature until it begins to thicken.
5. Pour the mixture over the lady fingers. Cool in the refrigerator for at least 2 hours before serving.

Mexican Chicken Casserole

 Serves 3

Total Cost: $4.13

2 boneless, skinless chicken breasts

½ small onion

6 flour tortillas

¾ cup grated Cheddar cheese

5½-ounces cream of mushroom condensed soup

5½-ounces can cream of chicken condensed soup

½ cup sour cream

¼ cup canned chopped jalapeño peppers, drained (or 4 fresh jalapeños)

½ cup tomato salsa

Serve over a bed of lettuce with fresh Tostadas (see recipe to follow).

1. Preheat oven to 300°F.
2. Cut the chicken into 1-inch cubes. Peel the onion and grate using the fine side of a vegetable grater. Tear the tortillas into eighths.
3. Combine the onion, cheese, soups, sour cream, and jalapeños in a medium-sized bowl. Make layers in a casserole dish using ⅓ of the flour tortillas, soup mixture, chicken, then salsa. Repeat twice, in that order.
4. Cover and bake for 2 hours.

TOSTADAS

Makes 4–10 depending on tortilla size

Total Cost: $0.81

¼ cup vegetable oil

6–8 corn tortillas

¼ teaspoon salt

1. Spread the oil evenly over the bottom of a large frying pan. Preheat to medium-high temperature.
2. Place the tortillas in hot oil, 1 at a time, and fry until crisp. Flip the tortillas when one side is brown to ensure even cooking.
3. Sprinkle with salt while cooking.
4. Place on paper towels to drain.

Key Lime Chicken

 Serves 2

$ Total Cost: $2.96

½ chipotle chili pepper

3 key limes

⅛ cup lemon juice

⅛ cup orange juice

½ cup green tomato salsa

1 tablespoon vegetable oil

½ teaspoon salt

2 skin-on chicken breasts

This is wonderful served with refried beans or red rice.

1. Remove and discard the rind from 2 of the key limes. Remove and discard the stem and seeds from the chili pepper.
2. Combine the peeled key limes, chili pepper, lemon juice, orange juice, salsa, oil, and salt in a blender or food processor. Blend on medium until you have a nice purée—it should be thick with no obvious chunks.
3. Transfer the blend to a medium-sized pot and cook on medium heat for about 15 minutes. Let cool.
4. Debone the chicken breasts and place in a large mixing bowl. Pour the sauce over the top. Cover and refrigerate for 6 to 12 hours.
5. Preheat the broiler. (These also are great cooked on the grill.)
6. Place on the broiler and use the marinate to baste the chicken every few minutes. Turn the chicken over when the first side gets brown and cook again. Chicken breasts take from 10 to 20 minutes to cook thoroughly. Cut into the center of 1 of the breasts to make sure it is cooked through before serving.
7. Cut the remaining key lime in half. Before serving, squeeze the juice of ½ a lime onto each breast.

The Chipotle Chili

Chipotle chilies are dried, smoked red jalapeño peppers. There is no other chili pepper like them. Although spicy, the flavor that lingers is the smoky taste. As a result, you should know what you are doing when you put them into a dish. They will flavor something more than any other chili pepper.

Jalapeño Chicken

 Serves 2

1 (1- to 2-pound) whole chicken

2 garlic cloves

2 fresh jalapeño peppers

½ cup orange juice

½ cup honey

⅛ cup lime juice

½ teaspoon cayenne pepper

½ teaspoon salt

Serve this with simple rice and vegetable dishes so you don't detract from the complex flavors in the chicken.

1. Preheat oven to 350°F.
2. Wash the chicken and cut it into eight serving pieces.
3. Remove the skin from the garlic. Remove the stem and seeds from the jalapeño peppers.
4. Put the garlic, peppers, orange juice, honey, lime juice, salt, and cayenne pepper in a blender or food process; blend on medium setting for 5 minutes or until the peppers and garlic are well chopped up.
5. Place the chicken in a roasting pan. Brush the glaze on the chicken liberally but save about half for later.
6. Cook for 1½ hours. After 30 minutes, turn the chicken and again glaze liberally. After another 30 minutes, turn the chicken over again and use the remaining glaze.

Chicken Tacos

 Serves 3

3 cups water
½ medium-sized yellow onion
2 garlic cloves
½ carrot
½ green bell pepper
½ celery rib

2 chicken breasts (with skin and bones)
½ teaspoon salt
½ teaspoon black pepper
6 flour tortillas

Authentic Mexican tacos are usually served with just meat and salsa. However, you can add the American fixing such as cheese and lettuce if you'd like.

1. Place the water in a large stockpot and bring to a boil.
2. Remove the skin from the onion and cut into 1-inch pieces. Remove the skin from the garlic cloves and cut into thin slices. Peel the carrot and cut into ½-inch rounds. Remove the core and seeds from the green pepper and cut into 1-inch pieces. Cut the celery into 1-inch pieces.
3. Place the chicken breasts, onion, garlic, carrot, green pepper, salt, black pepper and celery in the boiling water; boil for 20 minutes. Skim the foam from the top, reduce heat to medium, and continue cooking until the meat falls off the bones when picked up with a fork.
4. Pour the contents of the stockpot into a strainer. Pull out the chicken breasts. Remove the bones and skin. Discard all the vegetables, chicken bones, and skin.
5. Shred the meat. Use as a filling for the tacos.

Fruit and More Fruit
Being a warm-weather culture, Mexican dishes frequently use a great deal of fresh fruits. Although those in the United States tend to think of tropical fruits as distinctly Mexican, it's only because most of us don't get them that often. Berries and citrus fruits are common in Mexican diets, too.

Marinated Chicken

Serves 2

½ (2½ pounds) fryer chicken

¼ cup canned or frozen sliced
  carrots

½ celery stalks

½ medium white onion

¼ garlic clove

½ cup vegetable oil

¹⁄₁₆ teaspoon thyme

¹⁄₁₆ teaspoon marjoram

¼ bay leaf

3 peppercorns

¼ teaspoon salt

¾ cup vinegar

Serve cold, garnished with pickled vegetables.

1. Cut chicken into 2 serving pieces. Thaw the frozen carrots
   or drain canned carrots. Chop the celery into 1-inch pieces.
   Peel the onion and cut into 1-inch pieces. Peel and mince
   the garlic.
2. Heat the oil to medium temperature in a large skillet. Brown
   the chicken pieces, then place them in a large pot. Top with
   the carrots, onions, celery, garlic, thyme, marjoram, bay leaf,
   peppercorns, and salt. Pour the vinegar over the top.
3. Remove from heat and let cool to room temperature. Cover
   and refrigerate for 3 to 4 hours.

Chicken Chalupas

Serves 3

Total Cost: $3.64

6 corn tortillas

½ cup chicken stock

½ pound Monterey jack cheese

½ cup sour cream

1 cup Spicy Chicken (Chapter 2)

½ teaspoon paprika

Serve with a fresh spinach salad and Fruit Compote (see recipe to follow).

1. Soak the tortillas in ¼ cup of the stock. Grate the cheese.
2. Combine the remaining chicken stock with the sour cream.
3. Layer the ingredients in a casserole as follows: single layer of soaked tortillas, Spicy Chicken, sour cream mixture, cheese. Repeat until all the ingredients are used. Sprinkle with paprika.
4. Cover and refrigerate at least 8 hours.
5. Preheat oven to 350°F. When the oven is heated, bake the dish, uncovered, for 1 hour.

FRUIT COMPOTE

Serves 4

Total Cost: $1.51

¾ cup seedless green grapes

¾ cup fresh strawberries

1 medium orange

2 medium kiwi

1 medium peach

2½ tablespoons confectioners' sugar

1½ tablespoons Triple Sec or Cointreau liqueur

1½ tablespoons tequila

¾ tablespoon lime juice

1. Cut the grapes in half. Remove the stems from the strawberries and cut the fruit in half. Peel the oranges and slice into ¼-inch rounds. Peel the kiwis and slice into ¼-inch rounds. Peel the peaches, remove the pits, and cut into ¼-inch-thick slices.
2. In a small jar, combine the sugar, liqueur, tequila, and lime juice. Cover and shake until well mixed. Combine all the fruit in a large serving bowl and toss to mix. Add the dressing and toss the fruit until well covered. Cover and refrigerate for at least 4 hours before serving.

Traditional Pollo Verde

Serves 2

½ medium-sized white onion
½ garlic clove
1 tomatillo
½ bunch fresh parsley
½ cup green chili sauce

½ teaspoon salt
½ teaspoon ground white pepper
½ fryer chicken

Serve with Zesty Cheese Salad (see recipe to follow).

1. Peel the onion and cut into quarters. Peel the garlic. Remove the stems and peels from the tomatillo, then cut in half. Remove the stems from the parsley and roughly chop the leaves.
2. Combine the onion, garlic, tomatillo, parsley, chili sauce, salt, and white pepper in a blender or food processor; blend until liquefied.
3. Rinse the chicken and arrange in a large frying pan. Pour the sauce over the top. Cover and bring to boil. Reduce heat to low and simmer for about 1 hour or until chicken is tender.

ZESTY CHEESE SALAD

 Serves 3

½ small-sized red onion

1 garlic clove

½ small poblano chili

½ medium avocado

¼ medium jicama

⅙ cup fresh cilantro leaves

¼ pound mozzarella cheese

¼ teaspoon ground cumin

⅛ teaspoon fresh oregano (or ¼ teaspoon dry)

⅔ cup olive oil

⅙ teaspoon salt

⅛ teaspoon ground black pepper

⅛ cup lime juice

1. Peel the onion and cut into ¼-inch pieces. Peel and mince the garlic. Remove the stem and seeds from the chilies and cut into ¼-inch pieces. Peel and pit the avocado and slice into 2-inch lengths about ¼-inch thick. Peel the jicama and cut into pieces about the size of matchsticks. Remove the stems from the cilantro and chop the leaves into ¼-inch pieces. Cut the mozzarella into ½-inch cubes.
2. In a large mixing bowl, combine the onion, chilies, avocado, jicama, and cheese; toss until well mixed.
3. In a medium-sized container with a lid, combine the garlic, cumin, oregano, olive oil, salt, black pepper, and lime juice. Cover and shake until well mixed.
4. Pour the dressing over the vegetables and cheese; toss lightly.

How to Substitute Dry Spices

Because dry spices have the water taken out of them, you usually substitute half the amount of dry for the fresh variety. However, many spices lose their flavor when dried, so it's best to use what the recipe calls for if at all possible.

Southwestern Fried Chicken

 Serves 2

1½ pieces white bread

½ bunch fresh cilantro

1 garlic clove

1 egg

1 tablespoon masa harina or cornmeal

1 tablespoon pine nuts

¼ teaspoon ground cumin

¾ teaspoon dried oregano

¼ teaspoon salt

⅛ teaspoon cayenne pepper

1/16 teaspoon ground cloves

1 tablespoon prepared yellow mustard

½ tablespoon water

1 teaspoon honey

2 chicken breasts

⅛ teaspoon ground black pepper

1 tablespoon butter

Serve with Calabacitas (see recipe to follow) for a well-balanced, slightly spicy meal.

1. Preheat oven to 400°F.
2. Tear the bread into 1-inch pieces. Remove the stems from the cilantro. Peel the garlic. Separate the egg and discard the yolk.
3. Blend together the bread, cilantro, garlic, cornmeal, pine nuts, cumin, oregano, ⅛ teaspoon of the salt, cayenne pepper, and cloves in a food processor or blender until you have fine crumbs. Add the egg white and mix until the crumbs are moist. Spread out the crumb mixture on a large plate.
4. Mix together the mustard, water, and honey in a small bowl. Brush over the chicken with a pastry brush. Sprinkle the chicken with the pepper and remaining salt. Dip the chicken 1 piece at a time in the bread mixture, pressing slightly so the mixture sticks.
5. Melt the butter in a 9" × 11" baking dish. Place the chicken breasts skin-side down in the butter; bake for 20 minutes. Flip the chicken and bake for an additional 20 minutes.

Masa Harina

Masa harina is flour made from dried corn dough that is then ground into a powder. Although similar to cornmeal, it does have a subtly different texture and taste because of the double-grinding process. You can usually substitute cornmeal in most recipes, although masa harina will give a more authentic flavor and texture.

The $5 Takeout Cookbook

CALABACITAS (ZUCCHINI WITH CHEESE AND CORN)

 Serves 2

1½ small zucchini

1 medium red tomato

1 fresh jalapeño pepper

½ garlic clove

¼ pound mild Cheddar cheese

1 cup canned whole-kernel corn

1. Cut the zucchini into 1-inch chunks. Chop the tomatoes into ¼-inch pieces. Remove the stems and seeds from the jalapeños and chop into ¼-inch pieces. Peel and mince the garlic. Cut the cheese into ½-inch chunks.
2. Combine the squash, tomatoes, peppers, and garlic in a large saucepan. Turn heat to medium-low. Heat slowly until the ingredients are hot.
3. Add the corn and cheese. Cover and continue to cook until the cheese is melted.

Enchiladas Rancheros

 Serves 2

½ garlic clove

½ medium-sized yellow onion

½ fresh jalapeño pepper

1 large red tomato

½ tablespoon vegetable oil

¼ teaspoon dried oregano

¾ cup cooked chicken

¼ pound Monterey jack cheese

3 ounces fresh button mushrooms

1 cup sour cream

8 flour tortillas

Garnish with sour cream, guacamole, and chopped green onions.

1. Preheat oven to 350°F.
2. Peel and mince the garlic and onions. Remove the stems and seeds from the jalapeños and cut into ¼-inch pieces. Peel the tomatoes and chop into ½-inch pieces.
3. Heat the vegetable oil to medium temperature in a medium-sized frying pan. Add the garlic, onion, and jalapeño peppers; sauté until the onion is transparent. Add the tomatoes and oregano; cook for about 5 minutes, stirring frequently.
4. Cut the cooked chicken into ½-inch cubes. Grate the cheese. Clean the mushrooms and slice thinly.
5. Mix together the chicken, cheese, and mushrooms. Stir in the sour cream.
6. Put 3 to 4 tablespoons of filling into each tortilla. Roll up and place into a 9" × 13" baking dish. Pour the sauce over the top.
7. Bake for 30 minutes or until heated through.

Mushrooms

Different mushrooms have very different tastes. Don't hesitate to substitute exotic dried mushrooms such as wood ear, enoki, and porcini even if the recipe calls for fresh mushrooms.

The $5 Takeout Cookbook

Cozumel Chicken

Serves 2

💲 Total Cost: $2.94

2 large boneless chicken breasts

2 key limes

½ lemon

¼ cup orange juice

¼ tablespoon butter

¼ cup red chili sauce

Serve with grilled corn on the cob and fruit compote.

1. Preheat oven to 325°F.
2. Melt the butter on medium heat in a large skillet. Add the chicken breasts and cook until brown on 1 side. Flip and brown the other side.
3. Wash the limes and lemons but do not peel. Slice as thinly as possible.
4. Transfer the chicken to an ovenproof baking dish. Top with the lime and lemon slices. Pour the orange juice over the top.
5. Cover with aluminum foil and bake for about 1 hour or until the chicken is tender.
6. Remove the lime and lemon slices and pour the chili sauce over the chicken. Heat for 5 more minutes.

Key Limes Go

Mexicans love key lime juice in almost everything. They squirt fresh key lime juice into soups, onto salty tostadas, and into their drinking water. The secret is that key limes—tiny golf-ball–sized fruits—are actually very sweet and mild tasting as compared to the Florida and California limes that people in the United States are used to.

White Chili

Serves 2

¼ pound dry navy beans

3 cups chicken stock

½ garlic clove

¼ medium onion

1 cup cooked chicken, light and dark meat

½ (4-ounce) can green chilies

½ teaspoon ground cumin

⅜ teaspoon dried oregano

⅛ teaspoon ground cloves

¹⁄₁₆ teaspoon cayenne pepper

Top the chili with Monterey jack cheese, crushed tortilla chips, and a dollop of sour cream.

1. Soak the beans in 4 cups water for 2 to 10 hours.
2. Place the stock in large pot on low heat. Add the beans.
3. Remove the skin from the garlic and onions. Chop into ¼-inch pieces and add to the pot.
4. Remove the skin from the chicken and dice into ½-inch cubes. Add to the pot.
5. Add the remaining ingredients; stir well.
6. Simmer for 3 hours.

Substitute Mushrooms

To turn any meat dish into an instant vegetarian entrée, substitute morel mushrooms for the meat. Be sure to substitute by volume, not weight, because even these heavier mushrooms weigh less than meat.

Rice and Chicken with Guacamole

 Serves 2

1 large chicken breast

½ tablespoon vegetable oil

¾ cup dry white rice

½ cup frozen peas

1 small-sized yellow onion

1½ celery ribs

⅛ cup canned pimientos

½ teaspoon salt

½ teaspoon ground black pepper

½ cup mayonnaise

¾ teaspoon Tabasco or other hot sauce

½ large avocado

¼ teaspoon Worcestershire sauce

½ cup sour cream

¼ teaspoon dried onion flakes

¼ teaspoon garlic salt

¼ teaspoon onion salt

1. Remove the skin and bones from the chicken breasts. Bring the vegetable oil to medium temperature in a medium-sized frying pan. Add the chicken breasts and cook until the meat is lightly browned on all sides. Cut the breasts with a knife to make sure they are thoroughly cooked. Set on a paper towel to cool.
2. In a medium-sized pan, bring 3 cups water to a boil. Add the rice; boil for 5 minutes, then lower temperature to low. Cover and simmer for 20 minutes. Drain off excess water.
3. Cut the chicken breast into 1-inch cubes. Thaw the peas. Peel the onion and cut into ½-inch pieces. Cut the celery into ¼-inch pieces. Drain the pimientos and cut into ¼-inch pieces.
4. In a large serving bowl, combine the rice, chicken, peas, onion, celery, pimientos, salt, black pepper, ¼ cup of the mayonnaise, and ½ teaspoon of the hot sauce; toss lightly until well mixed.
5. Peel the avocado and then remove pit. Mash until no chunks remain.
6. Combine the avocado, remaining ¼ cup mayonnaise, Worcestershire sauce, sour cream, onion flakes, garlic salt, onion salt, and the remaining ¼ teaspoon hot sauce; mix well.
7. Pour the dressing over the salad and mix until all the ingredients are covered. Cover and refrigerate for at least 4 hours before serving.

Arroz con Pollo

 Serves 4

$ Total Cost: $2.80

1 small fryer chicken	2 tablespoons shortening
1 teaspoon salt	¾ cup uncooked brown rice
½ medium onion	½ teaspoon black pepper
2 large tomatoes	½ teaspoon cumin seeds
½ garlic clove	1–2 cups warm water

Add 1 chopped pepper of your choice to the recipe to make a spicier version of this meal.

1. Cut the chicken into 8 serving pieces. Sprinkle the salt over the chicken pieces. Remove the skin from the onion and slice into ¼-inch rings. Cut the tomatoes into eighths. Remove the skin from the garlic and mince.
2. Melt the shortening in a large frying pan over medium heat. Add the rice and stir constantly until the rice is browned.
3. In a separate frying pan, brown the chicken over medium heat.
4. Place the chicken pieces over the top of the rice. Add the tomatoes, onion, garlic, spices, and warm water.
5. Cover and simmer over low heat until the rice is tender and fluffy. If the mixture dries before the rice is cooked, add more warm water.

The Types of Arroz

Arroz is simply the Spanish word for "rice." As with most other warm-weather cultures around the world, the Mexicans have adopted rice as a staple of their diet. Although they usually use white rice in their cooking, brown rice is favored when seeking a more hearty dish.

Yucatan Tamale Pie

 Serves 3

¼ cup lard

1½ cup masa harina or cornmeal

1 medium white onion

1 garlic clove

2 jalapeño chilies

2 medium-sized ripe tomatoes

1 (1- to 2-pound) whole chicken

2 cups chicken stock

½ teaspoon dried oregano

⅛ teaspoon dried cilantro

¼ teaspoon brown sugar

For a stronger flavor, remove the vegetables from the stockpot and drain the liquid. Mix the vegetables with the chicken pieces when placing them in the casserole.

1. Preheat oven to 350°F.
2. Combine the lard and cornmeal, adding small amounts of water until the dough is soft enough to work with. Grease an ovenproof casserole dish and line the bottom and sides with the dough.
3. Remove the skin from the onion and garlic cloves; chop into ¼-inch pieces. Remove the stem and seeds from chilies and chop into ¼-inch pieces. Cut the tomatoes into 1-inch pieces.
4. Place the chicken, onions, garlic, chilies, tomatoes, stock, oregano, cilantro, and brown sugar into a large stockpot. Bring to a boil. Reduce heat to medium and simmer, covered, for 1 hour.
5. Remove the chicken and let cool. Reserve the broth. Remove the bones and skin from the chicken and tear the meat into strips about 1 inch wide. Layer the chicken on the dough in the casserole.
6. Bake, covered, for 1 hour. Pour 1 cup of the broth over the pie before serving.

Try Turkey

For a lean alternative in your next chicken recipe, substitute turkey. It has much less fat and much more protein than chicken while often being a better per-pound buy at the grocery store.

CHAPTER 2

BEEF

Empanaditas de Carne

 Serves 2

¼-pound beef roast

¼-pound pork roast

¾ cup flour

¼ teaspoon baking powder

½ teaspoon salt

¼ cup, plus 1 tablespoon, granulated sugar

¾ tablespoons shortening

1 egg

¼ cup water

¼ cup raisins

½ cup applesauce

¼ teaspoon ground cinnamon

⅛ teaspoon crushed cloves

⅛ cup chopped pecans

1 cup vegetable oil

These are just as good cold as they are hot. They go great in a sack lunch, too.

1. Put the beef roast and pork roast in a pot and add just enough water to cover the meat. Cover the pot and turn heat to medium. Simmer until the meat is completely cooked, at least 1 hour. Do not discard the cooking liquid.
2. Combine the flour, baking powder, ¼ teaspoon salt, and 1 tablespoon sugar. Blend in the shortening.
3. Beat the egg in a separate bowl and slowly add to the flour mixture. Add the water and mix to form a dough. Roll out the dough to about ⅛-inch thick and cut with a biscuit cutter.
4. Remove the meat from the bones. Discard the bones and grind the meat with a meat grinder or food processor. Place the meat in a large pot. Add the raisins, applesauce, ¼ cup sugar, cinnamon, cloves, ¼ teaspoon salt, and ⅛ cup chopped pecans. Mix to combine, adding enough of the cooking liquid from the meat to thoroughly moisten the mixture.
5. Simmer, uncovered, for 15 minutes, adding more water if the mixture seems dry. Make sure the mixture holds together, though; it should not be runny.
6. Put about 3 tablespoons of meat mixture in the center of each of the biscuits. Fold over and pinch the edges shut.
7. Heat the oil in a large frying pan until medium hot. Add several empanaditas. Fry on both sides until golden brown. Place on paper towels to cool.

Enchiladas

Serves 2

$ Total Cost: $4.85

½ cup tomato salsa

6 corn tortillas

1½ cup refried beans

1 cup grated Monterey jack cheese

¾ cup red or green chili sauce

Experiment until you find your own favorite ingredients. Try mixing beans and meat or adding Spicy Chicken (see recipe to follow). Or, for a cheesy enchilada, mix 3 different cheeses and don't include meat or beans.

1. Preheat oven to 375°F. Ladle ½ cup of the salsa into a 9" × 12" baking pan.
2. Put ¼ cup of the beans in the center of each tortilla. Add 2 tablespoons shredded cheese. Roll up and place in baking pan.
3. When all the enchiladas are in the baking pan, cover with the remaining sauce and cheese. Bake for 15 to 20 minutes.

SPICY CHICKEN

Yields 2 cups

$ Total Cost: $3.84

½ garlic clove

1 medium tomatoes

¾ fresh jalapeño chili peppers

¼ bunch fresh cilantro

¼ bay leaf

½ teaspoon salt

½ teaspoon ground black pepper

2-ounces Italian salad dressing

¼ fryer chicken (about 2½ pounds)

1. Peel and mince the garlic. Cut the tomatoes into 1-inch pieces, reserving the juice. Remove the stems and seeds from the chili peppers. Remove the stems from the cilantro.
2. Combine all the ingredients in a heavy pot. Cover and cook over medium heat for about 5 hours.
3. Remove the meat from the broth and let cool. Remove and discard the skin and bones, and shred the meat with forks or in a food processor. Discard the broth.

Burritos

Serves 2

½ cup refried beans

½ cup red rice

½ cup Shredded Beef (see recipe to follow)

¼ pound Cheddar cheese

½ cup tomato salsa

4 flour tortillas

¼ cup red chili sauce

⅛ cup sour cream

⅛ cup guacamole

Burritos are the "Poor Boy" sandwich of Mexico. They literally contain whatever is leftover from yesterday. Don't hesitate to add olives, lettuce, or even yesterday's ham.

1. Heat the beans, rice, and beef separately on low heat. Shred the cheese.
2. Add ¼ cup of the beans, ¼ cup beef, ¼ cup rice, and 1 tablespoon salsa to the middle of each tortilla. Drizzle 1 teaspoon of chili sauce on top. Roll up.
3. Top each burrito with a dollop of sour cream and a dollop of guacamole.

SHREDDED BEEF

Yields 1 cup

¼ garlic clove

½ medium tomato

⅜ fresh jalapeño chili pepper

⅛ bunch fresh cilantro

⅛ bay leaf

½ pound round steak

¼ teaspoon salt

¼ teaspoon ground black pepper

1-ounce Italian salad dressing

1. Peel and mince the garlic. Cut the tomatoes into 1-inch pieces, reserving the juice. Remove the stems and seeds from the chili peppers. Remove the stems from the cilantro.
2. Place all the ingredients in a heavy pot. Cover and cook over medium heat for about 5 hours.
3. Remove the meat from the broth, let cool, and cut into 2-inch cubes. Shred with forks or in a food processor. Discard broth.

Chili Rellenos

 Serves 3

3 large Anaheim chilies

¼ pound Mozzarella cheese

½ small white onion

⅛ cup canned jalapeño peppers, or 2 fresh jalapeños

1 cup canned tomatoes, with juice

¼ tablespoon olive oil

1 cup chicken stock

1 tablespoon cornstarch

1 egg

1 cup masa harina or cornmeal

½ teaspoon salt

1. Preheat oven to 350°F. Place the Anaheim peppers in the oven. Turn them when the tops are white. When both sides are white, remove the peppers and put them in a paper bag. Close the bag tightly, and let the peppers cool. (This makes it easier to peel off the skin.) Peel the skin from the peppers.
2. Cut the cheese into wedges about ½ inch wide. Stuff the wedges into the chilies.
3. Peel the onion and chop into ¼-inch pieces. Drain the jalapeño peppers and cut into ¼-inch pieces. Chop the tomatoes into ¼-inch pieces, reserving the juice.
4. In a medium-sized saucepan, heat the olive oil to medium temperature. Add the onions and sauté until the onions are brown. Add the chopped chilies and tomatoes with their juice. Add the stock and cornstarch; sauté on medium heat, stirring constantly until the sauce is the consistency of gravy.
5. Beat egg, then combine with the cornmeal or masa harina; mix well. If the mixture is not sticky, add water until it is about the consistency of thick pancake batter.
6. Dip the peppers into the egg and cornmeal batter.
7. Put the peppers into a lightly greased frying pan on medium heat. Brown the peppers on all sides.
8. Cover with sauce before serving.

Bell Peppers

Bell peppers have different flavors depending on their color. Green is the most acidic and sour tasting. Red has the most peppery flavor. Yellow and orange have a gentle flavor. Combine them to create unique flavors and a beautiful dish.

The $5 Takeout Cookbook

Beef Tamales

 Serves 3

9 large, dry corn husks

¼ cup lard

1 cup dehydrated masa harina

1 cup chicken stock

1 cup Shredded Beef (Chapter 2)

Serve with coleslaw.

1. Wash the corn husks in warm water. Place in a saucepan and cover with boiling water. Let soak for at least 30 minutes before using.
2. Beat the lard until light and fluffy. Gradually beat in the masa harina and stock until the dough sticks together and has a pastelike consistency.
3. Shake excess water from each softened corn husk and pat dry on paper towels. Spread about 2 tablespoons of dough on the center portion of each husk. Spoon about 1½ tablespoons beef onto the dough. Wrap the tamale, overlapping the sides and then folding up the top and bottom.
4. Lay the tamales in the top section of a double boiler with the open husk flaps on the bottom. Steam over simmering water for about 1 hour or until the corn husk can easily be peeled from the dough.

Using a Double Boiler

A double boiler consists of two pots, one sitting on top of the other. The food to be cooked goes in the top pot while the boiling water goes in the bottom. The steam from the boiling water cooks the food. By not having direct contact with the heat source, you eliminate the possibility of burning the food, while still being able to get it very hot.

Beef Flautas

Serves 4

8 corn tortillas

1½ cup Shredded Beef (Chapter 2)

1½ cups shredded Colby cheese

½ cup vegetable oil

Flautas can be made with spicy chicken meat, ground beef, or pork.

1. Place a tortilla on a flat surface; lay out another tortilla so that it overlaps the first tortilla about halfway.
2. Spoon about ⅓ cup of the shredded beef down the center length, where the tortillas overlap. Sprinkle about 2 tablespoons of cheese on top of the meat.
3. Roll up, starting with 1 long side and rolling toward the other. Pin closed with wooden picks or small skewers.
4. Repeat with the remaining tortillas, beef, and cheese to make 8 flautas.
5. Heat the oil to medium-high in a large frying plan. Fry each flauta until golden brown on both sides.

The $5 Takeout Cookbook

Beef Mole

 Serves 3

💲 Total Cost: $4.29

1½ pounds stewing beef

1½ fresh jalapeño peppers

1 medium-sized white onion

1 garlic clove

1½ medium-sized red tomato

1½ tablespoon vegetable oil

2 medium potatoes

½ medium zucchini (about 10 inches long)

1 teaspoon salt

½ teaspoon ground black pepper

When fresh vegetables are in season, don't hesitate to add carrots, corn, or any of your favorite vegetables to this dish.

1. Place the beef in a large saucepan and fill with water to about 2 inches from the top of the pan. Bring to a boil, cover, and reduce heat to medium. Cook for 2 hours. Drain and set aside.
2. Remove the stems and seeds from the jalapeños and cut into quarters. Remove the skin from the onion and cut into quarters. Remove the skin from the garlic cloves. Remove the skin from the tomatoes and cut into quarters. Place these ingredients in blender or food processor and blend on medium until all the ingredients are puréed. They should look as though they are chopped into very small pieces, but not blended into a paste.
3. Heat the oil on medium-high setting in a large frying pan. Add the purée and cook, stirring constantly for 5 minutes.
4. Peel the potatoes and cut into 1-inch cubes. Place in a medium-sized saucepan, cover with water, and boil until tender. Drain and set aside.
5. Cut the zucchini into 1-inch cubes.
6. Combine all the ingredients in a frying pan; stir gently. Heat on medium setting for 10 minutes.

Can You Really Eat a Mole?

Moles (pronounced *mo-LAY*) are actually stews made with thick, intensely flavorful sauces, usually featuring different chili peppers and nuts. Sometimes the mole is poured over uncut pieces of meat, such as chicken, so the meat can stew that way. Most often, however, the meat is cut up and made part of the sauce.

Fideo con Carne

 Serves 3

 Total Cost: $2.01

1 medium-sized red tomato
⅛ head cabbage
1½ garlic cloves
⅛ cup vegetable oil
4 ounces vermicelli noodles
½ pound lean ground beef

⅛ teaspoon ground cumin
⅛ teaspoon salt
⅛ teaspoon ground black pepper
1 quarts water

Serve with Pineapple and Coconut Salad (see recipe to follow).

1. Chop the tomatoes into ¼-inch pieces. Chop the cabbage into 1-inch pieces. Peel and mince the garlic.
2. Heat the oil to medium temperature in a large frying pan. Add the vermicelli noodles; sauté until the noodles are lightly browned. Remove the noodles and set aside.
3. In the same pan, sauté the garlic and until the beef is browned. Drain off the oil.
4. Add the tomatoes, vermicelli, cumin, salt, and ground pepper; stir until all the ingredients are mixed. Add the water. Bring to a simmer, cover, and cook for 10 minutes.
5. Add the cabbage and stir to combine. Simmer, uncovered, for 15 minutes.

PINEAPPLE AND COCONUT SALAD

Serves 4

$ Total Cost: $3.70

½ fresh pineapple (substitute canned if necessary)

½ fresh coconut (substitute 1 cups preshredded if necessary)

½ medium-sized fresh cabbage (substitute 1 cups preshredded if necessary)

½ cup mayonnaise

½ teaspoon lemon juice

3 large lettuce leaves

For a tropical change of pace, add 1 cup mango or fresh papaya to the salad.

1. Remove the rind, core, and top from the pineapple. Cut into ½-inch cubes. Remove the shell from the coconut and shred until you have 2 cups. Shred the cabbage until you have 2 cups.
2. Combine the pineapple, coconut, cabbage, mayonnaise, and lemon juice in a large serving bowl; toss gently until well mixed.
3. Cover and chill for at least 1 hour before serving. Serve by scooping onto lettuce leaves.

Taco Soup

 Serves 2

¼ large white onion

¼ green bell pepper

½ pound lean ground beef

¼ tablespoon paprika

¼ tablespoon chili powder

¼ tablespoon salt

¼ tablespoon ground black pepper

¾ 15-ounce can stewed tomatoes, with juice

¼ cup canned pinto beans, undrained

¼ cup canned kidney beans, undrained

¼ cup canned golden hominy, undrained

¼ cup canned whole-kernel corn, undrained

1½ cup water

1 Tostada (Chapter 1)

1. Peel the onion and chop into ¼-inch pieces. Remove the stem and seeds from the green pepper and chop into ¼-inch pieces.
2. Combine the onion, green pepper, ground beef, paprika, chili powder, salt, and ground black pepper in a large frying pan on medium heat. Cook until the ground beef is browned.
3. Add the ground beef mixture to a large stockpot. Add the stewed tomatoes, pinto beans, kidney beans, hominy, and whole kernel corn, along with all their liquids.
4. Stir, add the water, and bring to a boil. Turn the temperature to medium-low, cover, and simmer for 2 hours.
5. Top with crumbled tostadas right before serving.

Hominy

Hominy is actually dried white field corn that has been cooked with powdered lime until its skin falls off. The kernels' eyes are taken out and the kernel opens up until it resembles a piece of wet popcorn.

The $5 Takeout Cookbook

Pan-Fried Chimichangas

 Serves 2

½ medium-sized white onion

½ medium-sized red tomato

¼ cup canned jalapeño peppers, or 4 fresh jalapeños

¼ pound Colby cheese

⅓ pound lean ground beef

¾ teaspoon chili powder

¼ teaspoon ground black pepper

½ teaspoon garlic salt

⅛ teaspoon cayenne pepper

¼ teaspoon dried oregano

4 flour tortillas

½ cup vegetable oil

Serve with sour cream, guacamole, and tomato salsa.

1. Peel the onion and cut into ¼-inch pieces. Remove the stem from the tomato and cut into ¼-inch pieces. Chop the jalapeño peppers into ¼-inch pieces. Grate the cheese.
2. In a medium-sized frying pan, fry the ground beef and onions on medium heat until the meat is brown and the onions are translucent. Drain off the grease.
3. Add the tomatoes, jalapeños, chili powder, black pepper, garlic salt, chili powder, cayenne pepper, and oregano; simmer for 10 minutes.
4. Put 2 to 3 tablespoons of the mixture in the middle of each tortilla. Add 1 tablespoon of cheese on top. Fold the tortillas and secure with toothpicks.
5. Heat the vegetable oil to medium-high in a large skillet. Add 2 or 3 tortillas at a time. Fry quickly until golden brown on each side.

Taco Skillet Casserole

 Serves 3

Total Cost: $2.98

½ small yellow onion

½ garlic clove

⅛ head lettuce

4 corn tortillas

¾ pound ground beef

½ teaspoon salt

¼ teaspoon ground black pepper

½ teaspoon chili powder

1 cup canned tomato sauce

¼ cup vegetable oil

¼ cup grated Cheddar cheese

Add a side of Extraspecial Frijoles Refritos (Chapter 4).

1. Peel the onion and chop into ¼-inch pieces. Peel and mince the garlic. Shred the lettuce. Cut the tortillas into ½-inch-wide strips.
2. Crumble the ground beef into a large frying pan and brown on medium heat. Pour off excess fat.
3. Add the onion and garlic and cook for about 5 minutes longer, until the onion is soft; stir frequently.
4. Stir in the salt, pepper, chili powder, and tomato sauce, and continue cooking over low heat for about 15 minutes longer; stir frequently.
5. In a separate frying pan, heat the vegetable oil to medium-high. Fry the tortilla strips until crisp. Transfer to paper towels to absorb excess grease.
6. Stir the tortilla strips into the meat mixture and cook for about 5 minutes, stirring frequently.
7. Sprinkle with cheese. As soon as the cheese melts, remove from heat. Top with shredded lettuce and serve immediately.

Corn Husks as Spice

The Mexican culture is unique for using corn husks to spice food. Most often used in corn tamales, the husks are also used as a wrapper for other foods such as candy. Even when leaving the husk on for cooking the corn, you notice a distinctly earthy taste that is transferred to the food.

The $5 Takeout Cookbook

CHAPTER 3

VEGETABLE DISHES

Pastel de Elote (Corn Pie)

 Serves 3

Shortening

⅛ pound Monterey jack cheese

⅛ pound sharp Cheddar cheese

¼ cup canned jalapeño chili peppers

¾ cup frozen corn

¼ cup butter

2 medium eggs

15-ounce can cream-style corn

¼ cup masa harina or cornmeal

½ cup sour cream

¼ teaspoon salt

⅛ teaspoon Worcestershire sauce

This dish often is served as a side dish for meals such as Cinnamon Fried Chicken (see recipe to follow).

1. Preheat oven to 350°F. Grease a pie plate with shortening.
2. Cut the cheeses into ½-inch cubes. Drain the jalapeños and cut into ¼-inch pieces. Thaw the frozen corn. Melt the butter in a saucepan over low heat or in the microwave.
3. In a large mixing bowl, beat the eggs until frothy.
4. Add all the remaining ingredients; stir until thoroughly mixed. Pour into the prepared pie plate.
5. Bake for 20 minutes.

CINNAMON FRIED CHICKEN

 Serves 2

2 skin-on chicken breasts

½ cup milk

½ cup flour

1 tablespoon ground cinnamon

½ teaspoon cayenne pepper

½ tablespoon salt

½ teaspoon ground nutmeg

½ teaspoon ground cloves

2 tablespoons vegetable oil

If there is extra room in the roasting pan, wash potatoes, leaving the skin on, and quarter them. Place them in with the chicken to bake.

1. Preheat oven to 300°F
2. Wash the chicken thoroughly. Pour the milk into a soup bowl and dunk the chicken breasts in milk until completely coated. Discard the remaining milk.
3. In another soup bowl, mix together the flour, cinnamon, cayenne pepper, salt, nutmeg, and cloves. Roll each breast in the flour mixture until well coated.
4. Put the vegetable oil in a roasting pan. Place the chicken breasts skin-side down in the roasting pan and bake for 30 minutes.
5. Flip the chicken so that the skin side is up and put back in the oven for 1 hour.

Eggplant Casserole

Serves 3

$ Total Cost: $2.35

½ medium eggplant
¼ teaspoon garlic salt
¼ cup canned jalapeño
    peppers

1 cup canned tomato sauce
¼ cup sour cream
¼ teaspoon ground cumin
¾ cup grated Cheddar cheese

This goes very well as a side dish for Pork Roast with Apples (Chapter 1).

1. Preheat oven to 350°F.
2. Remove the stem from the eggplant. Wash the rind but do not peel. Slice into ½-inch-thick rounds. Arrange the rounds in a 9" × 9" lightly greased baking pan. Sprinkle with the garlic salt.
3. Combine the jalapeño peppers, tomato sauce, sour cream, and cumin; mix well. Pour over the eggplant rounds. Layer the cheese over the top.
4. Bake for 45 to 60 minutes or until the cheese is melted and the eggplant is soft.

Mexican Stuffed Peppers

Serves 2

$ Total Cost: $3.89

4 fresh, large jalapeño peppers
1–2 cups refried beans

⅛ cup shredded mild Cheddar
    cheese
½ tablespoon olive oil

1. Preheat oven to 300°F.
2. Remove the stems from the peppers and cut in half lengthwise. Remove the seeds.
3. Brush the cavities of the peppers with olive oil.
4. Place enough refried beans in each cavity to fill just to the top. (Don't heap the beans over the top.)
5. Sprinkle a small amount of cheese on top of each stuffed pepper.
6. Place on a baking sheet or in a baking pan. Bake for 30 minutes.

Mexican Roll-Ups

 Serves 3

💲 Total Cost: $2.05

1 fresh jalapeño chili pepper	¼ teaspoon garlic salt
½ bunch green onions	¼ teaspoon medium-hot red chili powder
¼ cup pitted black olives	
8 ounces cream cheese	3 flour tortillas

Serve with an assortment of fresh salsas for an interesting treat.

1. Remove the stems and seeds from the jalapeño peppers and chop the peppers into ¼-inch pieces. Remove the roots from the green onions and chop the onion and stems into ¼-inch pieces. Chop the olives into ¼-inch pieces.
2. Combine all the ingredients and mix until well blended.
3. Spread on tortillas. Roll up.

Green Onions and Scallions

Scallions are small yellowish onions that have a relatively mild flavor. Green onions are elongated white onions that grow no bigger than your index finger. It's common to eat the stems of green onions as you would chives.

Tomato Empanadas

 Serves 3

¼ pound butter

4 ounces cream cheese

1 cup flour

1 medium-sized red tomato

½ small yellow onion

These can be made ahead of time and frozen. They can be reheated in a microwave.

1. Mix together the butter and cream cheese until creamy. Add the flour and mix well.
2. Roll into a ball, cover, and chill for at least 4 hours.
3. Preheat oven to 350°F.
4. Cut the tomato into ¼-inch pieces. Peel the onion and cut into ¼-inch pieces. Mix together the tomato and onion.
5. Roll out the dough to about ¼-inch thick. Cut into circle about 3 inches across.
6. Put 1 teaspoon of tomato and onion mixture in the center of each circle. Fold in half and seal the edges with a fork. Prick the top of each empanada with a fork.
7. Place on a baking sheet and bake for 15 to 20 minutes.

Mexican Onion Soup

 Serves 3

$ Total Cost: $1.82

1½ large yellow onions

1 clove garlic

⅛ cup butter

1 cup tomato juice

1 cup beef broth (canned or homemade)

½ cup water

¼ cup tomato salsa

½ cup grated Monterey jack cheese

Serve with Brie and Papaya Quesadillas (see recipe to follow) for a light yet filling lunch.

1. Remove the skins from the onions and slice into thin rings. Remove the skin from the garlic cloves and mince.
2. Melt the butter over medium-low heat in a large frying pan. Add the onions and cook for about 20 minutes, stirring frequently. Onions should be tender and light brown.
3. Stir in the tomato juice, broth, water, and salsa. Bring to a boil. Reduce heat to low.
4. Simmer uncovered for 20 minutes. Top with grated cheese before serving.

Let's Hear It for Green Tomatoes

Although we tend to think of green tomatoes as unripe, therefore not fit to eat, the opposite is true. Because they have a firmer flesh and more tart taste, they add a distinctly different flavor from their ripe counterparts. Eating green tomatoes also means we get to enjoy the fresh garden tomatoes for a longer season.

BRIE AND PAPAYA QUESADILLAS

Serves 3

$ Total Cost: $4.77

¼ medium-sized yellow onion

1 large red chili pepper

½ ripe papaya

⅜ pound brie

¼ cup water

6 flour tortillas

2 tablespoons butter

2 tablespoons oil

1. Remove the peel from the onion and cut into ¼-inch-thick slices. Remove the stems from the chilies and dice the chilies into pieces about ⅛-inch square. Peel and deseed the papaya; dice into pieces about ⅛-inch square. Cut the brie into ¼-inch strips.
2. Heat the water on high in a medium-sized skillet until boiling. Remove from heat and add the onions; let stand for 10 to 15 minutes. Drain and set aside.
3. Warm the tortillas by placing them in the oven for 10 minutes at 250°F. Melt the butter in a small saucepan over low heat. Add the oil to the butter and stir until mixed. Remove the tortillas from the oven but leave the oven at 250°F.
4. Place a few strips of cheese on each tortilla. Add several onion strips, ¼ teaspoon of diced chili peppers, and 1 tablespoon of diced papaya. Add another tortilla to make a sandwich, then brush the top tortilla with the butter and oil mixture.
5. Place the quesadillas 1 at a time in a large skillet on medium heat. Brown both sides. Place the quesadillas on a baking sheet in the oven to keep warm while the others are being made.
6. Cut the quesadillas into 6 triangular wedges to serve.

Creamy Corn Soup

 Serves 2

¼ large white onion

¾ medium-sized red tomato

¾ cup canned (and drained) or frozen whole-kernel corn

1 cup chicken stock

¼ teaspoon salt

⅛ teaspoon ground black pepper

¼ cup heavy whipping cream

Garnish with strips of roasted red peppers to create a festive look and a unique combination of flavors.

1. Remove the skin from the onion and cut into quarters. Remove the skin from the tomatoes and cut into quarters.
2. Put the corn, onion, tomatoes, and ½ cup of the stock in a food processor or blender. Blend on medium setting for 3 minutes or until all the ingredients are melded. They do not have to be liquefied—small pieces of corn, onion, and tomato are fine.
3. Place the remaining stock in a large saucepan on medium-low heat. Stir in the blended mixture. Add the salt and pepper. Heat thoroughly, but do not boil.
4. Stir in the whipping cream and cook on low heat, stirring constantly, for 5 minutes.

Peeling Tomatoes

Although a tomato can be peeled cold, the easiest way to peel it is to drop it in boiling water for 20 seconds. Then cool it by running it under cold water. The peel will easily strip off with a paring knife.

CHAPTER 4

RICE AND BEANS

Arroz con Queso

Serves 2

1 cup dry white rice

6 ounces Monterey jack cheese

1 ounce Cheddar cheese

⅛ cup canned, diced green chilies

½ pint sour cream

Serve with Mexican Pot Roast (see recipe to follow).

1. Preheat oven to 350°F.
2. Bring 4 cups water to boil in a medium-sized saucepan. Add the rice; cover and boil for 5 minutes. Reduce heat to low and simmer for 20 minutes or until the rice is tender. Drain off any excess water.
3. Grate the cheeses. Drain the chilies and mix into the sour cream.
4. In a 1-quart casserole, layer the ingredients in the following order: ½ the rice, ½ the sour cream with jalapeños, the remaining rice, sour cream with jalapeños, and Monterey jack cheese.
5. Bake for 30 minutes. Top with Cheddar cheese and broil for 2 to 3 minutes before serving.

MEXICAN POT ROAST

 Serves 3

1½ tablespoon olive oil	3 medium-sized red tomatoes
1½-pound pot roast	2 fresh morita chilies
¼ cup flour	⅛ teaspoon dried oregano
½ large yellow onion	½ teaspoon salt
½ garlic clove	

Thicken the sauce by adding ¼ cup flour and cooking it on the stove until it becomes a gravy. Serve drizzled over the meat or over mashed potatoes.

1. Preheat oven to 350°F.
2. Heat the olive oil in a large skillet on medium. Dredge the beef in the flour by pounding the flour into the meat until no more flour will stick. Place the beef in the skillet. Cook, turning until the meat is brown on all sides.
3. Peel the onion and garlic clove. Cut the onion into ¼-inch-thick rings and mince the garlic. Cut the tomatoes into 1-inch pieces. Stem and seed the chilies and cut into ¼-inch pieces.
4. Place the pot roast in a roasting pan. Sprinkle with oregano and salt, and cover with the remaining ingredients.
5. Cook, covered, for 2 hours.

Casa Grande

Serves 3

¾ cup uncooked white rice

½ large bunch fresh spinach

½ large yellow onion

1 tablespoon butter

¾ cup Colby cheese

⅛ teaspoon garlic salt

2 eggs

¼ cup milk

1 teaspoon salt

¼ teaspoon ground black pepper

Serve with a crisp green salad and fresh fruit for a well-balanced meal.

1. Add the rice to 3 cups water in a medium-sized pan. Cover, bring to a boil, and cook for 5 minutes. Turn the heat to low and simmer for 20 minutes or until the rice is tender.
2. Remove the stems from the spinach and wash well. Pat dry. Place in a medium-sized pot with 1 cup water. Cover and cook on low heat until the spinach is limp and has diminished in size to about 1 cup. Drain off the water from spinach.
3. Preheat oven to 350°F.
4. Peel the onion and chop into ¼-inch pieces. In a large frying pan, melt the butter. Add the onion and cook until clear and tender but not brown. Add the rice, spinach, ½ cup of the cheese, and the garlic salt; mix well.
5. Combine the eggs, milk, salt, and pepper; mix well. Stir into the rice mixture.
6. Pour into a casserole dish and bake, uncovered, for 30 minutes.

Experimenting with Rice

There are many types of rice available in today's markets. Most are fairly easy to cook with, although you will need to experiment with the amount of water and cooking time each one needs. Generally, the less processed the rice, the more water it will take up and the more cooking time it will need.

Cold Rice and Beans

 Serves 3

¾ cup dry white rice

½ cup frozen peas

1 cup canned pinto beans

1 cup canned black beans

1½ celery ribs

½ medium-sized red onion

½ cup canned jalapeño chili peppers, or 4 fresh jalapeños

½ bunch fresh cilantro

⅛ cup white wine vinegar

⅛ cup olive oil

½ teaspoon salt

¼ teaspoon garlic powder

¼ teaspoon ground black pepper

⅛ teaspoon cayenne pepper

Serve as a summer luncheon with fresh flour tortillas and jasmine and rose hips tea.

1. Bring 3 cups water to boil in a medium-sized pot. Add the dry rice. Cover and boil for 5 minutes. Reduce heat to medium-low and simmer for 20 minutes. Drain off excess water.
2. Thaw the peas. Rinse and drain the beans. Cut the celery ribs into ¼-inch pieces. Peel the onion and cut into ¼-inch rounds. Drain the jalapeño peppers and cut into ¼-inch pieces. Remove the stems from the cilantro and roughly chop the leaves into ½-inch pieces.
3. Combine the rice, peas, pinto beans, black beans, celery, onion, jalapeño peppers, and cilantro in a large serving bowl; toss lightly to mix.
4. In a small glass jar, combine 2 tablespoons water, the white wine vinegar, olive oil, salt, garlic powder, black pepper, and cayenne pepper. Cover and shake until well mixed. Pour over the salad. Toss until all the ingredients are covered.
5. Cover and refrigerate for at least 24 hours before serving.

Extraspecial Frijoles Refritos

 Serves 3

1¼ cup uncooked pinto beans

3 slices bacon

1 small white onion

1 garlic clove

2 large tomatoes

½ teaspoon salt

½ teaspoon ground black pepper

½ teaspoon dried oregano

½ teaspoon ground cumin

½ cup beef broth

This is traditionally served with tortillas or dry toast triangles. However, it also makes an excellent meat substitute in tacos or enchiladas.

1. Soak the beans overnight in 5 cups of water. Drain and place in a large saucepan on medium heat. Add 4 cups of water. Cover and cook until tender but not mushy (about 2 hours). Remove from heat and drain.
2. In a large frying pan, fry the bacon until crisp. Set the bacon on a paper towel to drain grease. Chop roughly.
3. Remove the skin from the onion and chop into ¼-inch pieces. Remove the skin from the garlic and mince. Add the onion and garlic to the bacon grease and sauté on medium heat until golden brown.
4. Cut the tomatoes into ½-inch pieces. Add the tomatoes and beans to the onions and garlic in the frying pan; stir together. Add the salt, pepper, oregano, and cumin; mix thoroughly. Stir in the chopped bacon. Stir in the beef broth. Cover and simmer on medium-low heat for 20 minutes.

Black Bean and Avocado Burritos

 Serves 2

¼ cup dry black beans (or ½ cup canned black beans)

¼ cup dry brown rice

2 flour tortillas

½ small onion

½ medium avocado

⅛ cup canned or frozen whole-kernel corn

1 tablespoon fresh cilantro

⅛ cup canned green chilies or 2 fresh green chilies

⅛ teaspoon salt

¼ teaspoon black pepper

¼ cup shredded Monterey jack cheese

¼ cup tomato salsa

¼ cup shredded lettuce

Add diced chicken or shredded beef to the filling for a heartier meal. Serve with tortilla chips and Chili con Queso (see recipe to follow).

1. To cook the black beans, soak the dry beans in water overnight. Drain and rinse the beans. Bring 1½ cups of water to boil. Add the beans, cover, and boil for 5 minutes. Reduce heat to medium-low and cook for 1 hour. Drain off remaining water before using.
2. To cook the brown rice, bring 1½ cups of water to a boil. Add the rice. Cover and boil for 5 minutes. Reduce heat to medium-low and cook for an additional 30 minutes. Drain off remaining water before using.
3. Preheat oven to 350°F. Place the tortillas in a covered container in the oven for 5 to 10 minutes.
4. Remove the skin and chop the onion into ¼-inch pieces. Remove the skin and pit from the avocado and chop the avocado meat into ½-inch pieces. Drain or thaw the corn. Remove the stems from the cilantro and roughly chop the leaves. Roughly chop the lettuce.
5. Combine the beans, rice, onion, corn, cilantro, lettuce, green chilies, salt, and pepper in a medium sized-bowl. mix well.
6. Remove the tortillas from the oven and place ½ cup of the rice-bean mixture in the center of each tortilla. Top each with ¼ of the avocado, 2 tablespoons cheese, and 1 tablespoon salsa.
7. Roll up each tortilla. Fold over the ends before serving.

CHILI CON QUESO

 Serves 4

½ large-sized yellow onion

½ garlic clove

1½ fresh chipotle chili pepper

½ fresh jalapeño pepper

½ medium tomato

⅛ pound Monterey jack cheese

⅛ pound Colby cheese

½ tablespoon vegetable oil

¼ cup sour cream

This is the perfect dip for tortilla chips. It also makes an excellent sauce to pour over enchiladas.

1. Remove the skin from onions and garlic; chop into ¼-inch pieces.
2. Remove the stems and seeds from the peppers and chop into ¼-inch pieces.
3. Chop the tomatoes into ¼-inch pieces.
4. Grate the cheeses.
5. Heat the oil at medium temperature in a large skillet. Add the onions and garlic; sauté until tender but not brown. Add the peppers and tomatoes; cook for 3 minutes, stirring constantly.
6. Turn the heat to medium-low. Add the cheeses to the pan and cook, stirring constantly, until the cheese melts. Stir in the sour cream.

Mixed Bean Soup

Serves 2

$ Total Cost: $1.47

¼ cup each dried pinto, kidney, and black beans

1 small yellow onion

½ garlic clove

½ medium-sized red tomato

¼ large carrot

¼ fresh jalapeño or habanero pepper

¼ teaspoon chili powder

⅛ teaspoon red chili pepper flakes

½ teaspoon salt

½ cup chicken stock

Serve with fresh tortillas sprinkled with garlic salt.

1. Soak the beans overnight in 6 cups water.
2. Remove the skin from the onion and chop into ¼-inch pieces. Remove the skin from the garlic and mince. Remove the stems from the tomatoes and chop into ½-inch pieces. Peel the carrot and chop into ¼-inch pieces. Remove the stem and seeds from the pepper.
3. Add all the ingredients *except* the chicken stock to a large stockpot. Bring to a boil for 5 minutes. Reduce heat to medium-low and simmer, uncovered, for 3 hours.
4. Drain off the water and transfer the mixture to a blender. (You may need to divide it into 2 or 3 groups.) Blend on medium setting for 2 minutes or until the mixture becomes a paste.
5. Stir in the chicken stock. Reheat to serving temperature.

The $5 Takeout Cookbook

Bean Burritos

 Serves 3

1 teaspoon ground cumin

1½ cup refried beans

⅛ cup sour cream

½ cup tomato salsa

3 large flour tortillas

¼ cup grated Monterey jack cheese

Serve with fresh Tostadas (Chapter 1) and guacamole.

1. Place the cumin in a small frying pan on low heat. Heat until toasted and fragrant, stirring constantly.
2. Place the beans in a blender or food processor and blend on medium speed until smooth. Add the cumin and sour cream; blend until well mixed.
3. Remove from blender and stir in the tomato salsa.
4. Add about ⅔ cup of the mixture to the center of each tortilla. Sprinkle cheese on top. Fold over ends and roll up.

Stocking Up on Ethnic Staples

If your local grocery store doesn't carry certain ethnic spices or ingredients, you may be able to find them on the Internet or at specialty shops. Just make sure to stock up on shelf-stable necessities so you can make these dishes whenever you like.

Bean-Stuffed Peppers

 Serves 3

1 small egg

3 red bell peppers

1 cup refried beans

⅛ cup flour

½ cup shortening

¼ cup cream

⅛ pound Monterey jack cheese

Serve as a side dish for Jalapeño Chicken (Chapter 1).

1. Preheat oven to 350°F.
2. Separate the egg. Beat the egg yolk until thick. Beat the white until it is shiny and stiff. Fold the egg white into the egg yolk. Remove the stems and seeds from the bell peppers. Stuff with refried beans. Dust the peppers with flour, then dip into the egg mixture.
3. Melt the shortening in a medium-sized frying pan. Put 2 or 3 peppers in the pan at a time and fry on all sides.
4. Arrange the peppers in an ovenproof casserole dish. Cover with the cream. Grate the cheese and sprinkle on top. Bake for about 20 minutes or until the beans are hot.

Enrollados

 Serves 3

½ medium-sized yellow onion

1 medium-sized red tomato

1½ cup refried beans

½ cup red chili sauce

6 flour tortillas

¾ cup shredded Monterey jack cheese

¼ cup vegetable oil

1 egg

¼ cup flour

You can also add beef, chicken, or pork to these fried tacos. They're wonderful served with guacamole and various salsas for dipping.

1. Peel the onion and chop into ¼-inch pieces. Remove the stems from the tomatoes and chop into ¼-inch pieces.
2. Heat the beans on low in a medium-sized saucepan. Add the onion, tomatoes, and chili sauce; heat through.
3. Spoon about ⅓ cup of the mixture into the center of each tortilla. Add about 2 tablespoons of the cheese. Roll up the tortilla as you would an enchilada.
4. Heat the oil to medium-high in a large frying pan. Beat the eggs in a medium-sized bowl. Roll each tortilla in the flour and then in the beaten eggs. Place in the frying pan and fry until golden brown on all sides.

Canned or Fresh Peppers?

A stop at a local Wal-Mart in the northern United States found no fewer than seven varieties of fresh chili peppers—showing that you will likely be able to find fresh chilies to meet your needs virtually anywhere. However, if you must use canned, plan to use about half as much as you would of fresh, because they become more packed during the canning process.

Black Bean Soup

 Serves 4

1 cup dried black beans

1¼ quarts water

1 garlic clove

1 medium-sized yellow onion

¼ cup vegetable oil

¼ teaspoon salt

¼ teaspoon ground black pepper

⅛ teaspoon whole fennel seeds

⅛ teaspoon dried basil

½ teaspoon granulated sugar

½ teaspoon dried mustard

½ teaspoon grated lemon rind

⅛ teaspoon ground allspice

½ teaspoon dried cilantro

½ cup canned condensed tomato sauce

1½ tablespoon lemon juice

Garnish with grated Cheddar cheese and sour cream.

1. Soak the beans overnight in ½ quart of the water.
2. Remove the skin from the garlic and mince. Remove skin from the onions and cut into ¼-inch pieces. Put oil, onions and garlic in a medium frying pan on medium heat. Sauté until the onions are limp, not brown. Drain the oil.
3. Combine all the ingredients *except* the lemon juice in a large soup pot. Stir until well blended. Bring to a boil, then lower temperature to medium-low. Simmer, uncovered, for 2 hours or until the beans are soft.
4. Add the lemon juice and stir right before serving.

Beans Galore

Although we think of only a couple types of beans, there are many, many varieties that Mexicans routinely use. Traditional grocery stores are beginning to carry more of these varieties, but you also might try a local food co-op. Virtually any bean can be substituted in these recipes, depending on your taste.

The $5 Takeout Cookbook

PART TWO
THAI

Influenced by the many cultures including the Portuguese, Indonesians, Indians, and Chinese, Thai cuisine carefully balances sweet, salty, sour, bitter, and hot flavors in every meal. The key flavoring agents found in a Thai kitchen include coconut, lime, chili, garlic, ginger, cilantro, and dried fish (to make fish sauce). These ingredients are as basic as salt and pepper are to a Western kitchen.

The delicate blend of flavors may seem difficult to duplicate, but with these simple, delicious recipes, you'll never need to pull out that Thai takeout menu again!

CHAPTER 5

BEEF AND SEAFOOD

Bangkok-Style Roasted Beef Tenderloin

 Serves 2

½ teaspoon salt

⅛ teaspoon ground ginger

⅛ teaspoon ground cardamom

⅛–¼ teaspoon freshly ground black pepper

1 (1-pound) beef tenderloin, trimmed

Olive oil

¼ cup chicken, pork, or vegetable stock, or water

When I'm in a hurry, but still want a satisfying meal, this is it. While the tenderloins are roasting, I prepare a salad, some vegetables, and some rice or couscous. The whole dinner is ready in less than 30 minutes!

1. Place rack on bottom third of the oven, then preheat the oven to 500°F.
2. Combine the spices in a small bowl.
3. Rub the tenderloin with the spice mixture and a bit of olive oil. Place the tenderloin in a roasting pan and cook for 10 minutes.
4. Turn the tenderloin over and roast for 10 more minutes or until done to your liking.
5. Transfer the beef to a serving platter, cover with foil, and let rest.
6. Pour off any fat that has accumulated in the roasting pan. Place the pan on the stovetop over high heat and add the stock (or water). Bring to a boil, scraping the bottom of the pan to loosen any cooked-on bits. Season with salt and pepper to taste.
7. To serve, slice the tenderloin into thin slices. Pour a bit of the sauce over top, passing more separately at the table.

Thai-Style Beef with Broccoli

 Serves 2

2 tablespoons vegetable oil

1 medium shallot, chopped

1 teaspoon chili powder

1 tablespoon brown sugar

1 tablespoon fish sauce

1 tablespoon sweet soy sauce

1 tablespoon preserved
  soybeans (optional)

⅔ pound lean beef, cut into
  bite-sized pieces

2 cups water

½ of a 7–8 ounce package of
  rice sticks

1 cup broccoli pieces

Lime wedges (optional)

Hot sauce (optional)

To make this a vegetarian dish, omit the beef and use 3 cups of broccoli instead of only 1.

1. Heat the vegetable oil in a wok over medium-high heat. Add the shallot and stir-fry until it begins to soften. Add the chili powder and continue to stir-fry until well combined.
2. Add the brown sugar, fish sauce, soy sauce, and soybeans; Stir-fry for 30 seconds.
3. Add the beef and continue to stir-fry until the beef is almost done, approximately 2 minutes.
4. Stir in the water and bring it to a boil. Add the rice sticks, stirring until they start to cook. Reduce the heat to medium, cover, and let cook for 30 seconds. Stir and reduce the heat to medium-low, cover, and let cook for 3 minutes.
5. Add the broccoli pieces, cover, and cook for 1 minute. Remove the wok from the heat and adjust seasoning to taste.
6. Serve with wedges of lime and hot sauce passed separately at the table.

Grilled Ginger Beef

Serves 3

$ Total Cost: $4.93

4 cups low-salt beef broth

1 stalks lemongrass

1½ cloves garlic

1 (1-inch) piece ginger, cut in half

½ onion, cut in half

½ cinnamon stick

1 dried red chili pepper

½ (2-inch) piece of ginger, minced

½ small package of rice noodles

½ pound green vegetables

1 tablespoon (or to taste) soy sauce

¾ pound round steak

Salt and pepper to taste

3 scallions, minced

This may be my favorite recipe in this book. Its complex, aromatic overtones will make your taste buds beg for more. It's well worth the effort.

1. Place the beef broth, lemongrass, and garlic in a large pot; bring to a boil.
2. In the meantime, place the ginger and onion halves, cut-side down, in a dry skillet over high heat and cook until black. Add the onion and ginger to the broth mixture.
3. Place the cinnamon and dried chili peppers in the dry skillet and toast over medium heat for 1 minute; add to the broth mixture.
4. Reduce the heat and simmer the broth for 1 to 2 hours. Cool, strain, and refrigerate overnight.
5. Before you are ready to eat, remove the broth from the refrigerator and skim off any fat that may have accumulated. Bring the broth to a simmer and add the minced ginger.
6. Soak the rice noodles in hot water for 10 to 20 minutes or until soft; drain.
7. Blanch the vegetables for about a minute. Using a slotted spoon, remove them from the boiling water and shock them in cold water.
8. Season the broth to taste with the soy sauce. Season the steaks with salt and pepper and grill or broil to your liking.
9. To serve, slice the steak into thin strips (cutting across the grain) and place them in six large bowls. Add a portion of noodles and vegetables to the bowls and ladle the broth over the top.

Chiang Mai Beef

 Serves 2

Total Cost: $3.51

1½ cup water

1 cup uncooked long-grained rice

½ pound lean ground beef

2 tablespoons soy sauce

½ tablespoon vegetable oil

½ tablespoon chopped garlic

½ tablespoon small dried chilies

1 green onions, trimmed and sliced

Fish sauce

Chiang Mai is the principal city in Northern Thailand, known for its mountain scenery, fertile valleys, and hill tribe handicrafts. This is one of the main starting points for tourists interested in jungle treks, elephant rides, and orchid farms.

1. In a large saucepan, bring the water to a boil, then stir in the rice. Cover, reduce heat to low, and cook until the water is absorbed, about 20 minutes.
2. Put the cooked rice in a large mixing bowl and let cool to room temperature.
3. Add the ground beef and soy sauce to the rice, mixing thoroughly. (I find using my hands works best.)
4. Divide the rice-beef mixture into 8 to 12 equal portions, depending on the size you prefer, and form them into loose balls. Wrap each ball in foil, making sure to seal them well.
5. Steam the rice balls for 25 to 30 minutes or until cooked through.
6. While the rice is steaming, heat the vegetable oil in a small skillet. Add the garlic and the dried chilies and sauté until the garlic is golden. Transfer the garlic and the chilies to a paper towel to drain.
7. To serve, remove the rice packets from the foil and slightly smash them serving plates. Pass the garlic-chili mixture, the green onions, and the fish sauce separately to be used as condiments at the table.

Cinnamon Stewed Beef

 Serves 2

¾ quarts water

1 tablespoon sugar

1 whole star anise

1½ tablespoon soy sauce

½ clove garlic, smashed

1 tablespoon sweet soy sauce

½ (2-inch) piece of cinnamon stick

3 sprigs cilantro

½ celery stalk, sliced

½ pound beef sirloin, trimmed of all fat and cut into 1-inch cubes

½ bay leaf

Cinnamon is not a spice we Westerners typically use in savory dishes, but it is great at balancing spice or salt.

1. Place the water in a large soup pot and bring to a boil. Reduce heat to low and add the remaining ingredients.
2. Simmer, adding more water if necessary, for at least 2 hours or until the beef is completely tender. If possible, let the stewed beef sit in the refrigerator overnight.
3. To serve, place noodles or rice in the bottom of 4 soup bowls. Add pieces of beef and then ladle broth over. Sprinkle with chopped cilantro or sliced green onions if you like. Pass a vinegar-chili sauce of your choice as a dip for the beef.

Minty Stir-Fried Beef

 Serves 2

3–7 (to taste) serrano chilies, seeded and coarsely chopped

⅛ cup chopped garlic

⅛ cup chopped yellow or white onion

⅛ cup vegetable oil

½ pound flank steak, sliced across the grain into thin strips

1 tablespoon fish sauce

½ tablespoon sugar

¼–½ cup water

¼ cup chopped mint leaves

If the mint in this recipe is too pungent for your tastes, you can easily substitute cilantro, but I suggest being adventuresome and giving this a try. The beef in this recipe is also makes great fajitas!

1. Using a mortar and pestle or a food processor, grind together the chilies, garlic, and onion.
2. Heat the oil over medium-high heat in a wok or large skillet. Add the ground chili mixture to the oil and stir-fry for 1 to 2 minutes.
3. Add the beef and stir-fry until it just begins to brown.
4. Add the remaining ingredients, adjusting the amount of water depending on how thick you want the sauce.
5. Serve with plenty of Jasmine rice.

Peeling Garlic

To peel garlic, place the clove on a cutting board and smash it with the back or side of a knife, which will split the skin.

The $5 Takeout Cookbook

Cambodian Beef with Lime Sauce

 Serves 2

½ tablespoon sugar

1 teaspoon freshly ground black pepper, divided

1 tablespoon soy sauce

3 cloves garlic, crushed

¾ pound sirloin, trimmed and cut into bite-sized cubes

1 tablespoon lime juice

½ teaspoon water

1 tablespoon vegetable oil

This simple marinade is so good that even though the lime sauce is a breeze, the meat is equally good without it. If you don't have any beef on hand, use pork tenderloin instead.

1. In a bowl large enough to hold the beef, combine the sugar, 1 teaspoon of black pepper, soy sauce, and garlic. Add the beef and toss to coat. Cover and let marinate for 30 minutes.
2. In a small serving dish, combine the remaining black pepper, the lime juice, and the water; set aside.
3. In a large sauté pan, heat the vegetable oil over medium-high heat. Add the beef cubes and sauté for 4 minutes for medium-rare.
4. This dish may be served either as an appetizer or a main dish. For the appetizer, mound the beef on a plate lined with lettuce leaves with the lime sauce on the side. Use toothpicks or small forks to dip the beef into the lime sauce. For a main dish, toss the beef with the lime sauce to taste. Serve with Jasmine rice.

Seafood Stir-Fry

 Serves 2

3 tablespoons vegetable oil

3 teaspoons garlic, chopped

2 shallots, chopped

1 stalk lemongrass, inner core finely chopped

¼ cup chopped basil

1 can bamboo shoots, rinsed and drained

3 tablespoons fish sauce

Pinch of brown sugar

¼ pound fresh shrimp, scallops, or other seafood, cleaned

Rice, cooked according to package directions

When I'm in the seafood section of my favorite grocery store and everything looks great, I start thinking about this simple stir-fry. I buy a little of everything that strikes my fancy, go home, and have a seafood feast.

1. Heat the oil in a skillet or wok over high heat. Add the garlic, shallots, lemongrass, and basil, and sauté for 1 to 2 minutes.
2. Reduce heat, add the remaining ingredients, and stir-fry until the seafood is done to your liking, approximately 5 minutes.
3. Serve over rice.

Bamboo

Bamboo, a favorite of panda bears, is indigenous to Asia. However, bamboo is farmed in California and actually grows wild in some parts of Arizona!

The $5 Takeout Cookbook

Curried Shrimp with Peas

 Serves 2

$ Total Cost: $4.63

¾ teaspoon red curry paste

½ tablespoon vegetable oil

1 (7-ounce) can unsweetened coconut milk

2 teaspoons fish sauce

1–1½ teaspoons brown sugar

¼ pound large shrimp, peeled and deveined

½ cup packed basil leaves, chopped

½ cup packed cilantro, chopped

1 (5-ounce) package thawed frozen peas

Jasmine rice, cooked according to package directions

A beautifully colored curry—pink shrimp in a pink sauce peppered with green peas! I also appreciate the textures of the main ingredients. The shrimp and the peas have a freshness that perfectly complements the silkiness of the Jasmine rice.

1. In a large pot, combine the curry paste, vegetable oil, and ¼ cup of the coconut milk; cook over medium heat for 1 to 2 minutes.
2. Stir in the remaining coconut milk and cook for another 5 minutes.
3. Add the fish sauce and sugar, and cook for 1 minute more.
4. Add the shrimp, basil, and cilantro; reduce heat slightly and cook for 4 to 5 minutes or until the shrimp are almost done.
5. Add the peas and cook 2 minutes more.
6. Serve over Jasmine rice.

Shrimp Sizes

Shrimp are sized according to how many come in a pound. Medium means that there are about forty shrimp per pound. Large equals thirty, extra-large equals twenty-five, jumbo equals twenty, and colossal equals about fifteen. Salad shrimp are too tiny to count, so they are weighed instead.

Stir-Fried Shrimp and Green Beans

 Serves 2–3

1 tablespoon vegetable oil

1 tablespoon red curry paste

½ cup cleaned shrimp

1½ cups green beans, trimmed and cut into 1-inch lengths

2 teaspoons fish sauce

2 teaspoons sugar

The green beans are the stars of this simple stir-fry, but the shrimp are the highlight. They give the beans a bit more flavor and the dish more color and protein!

1. Heat the vegetable oil over medium heat. Stir in the curry paste and cook for 1 minute to release the fragrance.
2. Add the shrimp and the green beans at the same time, and stir-fry until the shrimp become opaque. (The green beans will still be quite crispy. If you prefer your beans softer, cook 1 additional minute.)
3. Add the fish sauce and the sugar; stir to combine.
4. Serve immediately with rice.

Lime-Ginger Fillets

 Serves 4

4 tablespoons unsalted butter, at room temperature

2 teaspoons lime zest

½ teaspoon ground ginger

½ teaspoon salt

4 fish fillets, such as whitefish, perch, or pike

Salt and freshly ground black pepper

These delicate fillets cook in a jiffy, so make sure to pay attention while they are under the broiler. Overcooking fish dries it out and causes it to loose its flaky texture.

1. Preheat the broiler.
2. In a small bowl, thoroughly combine the butter, lime zest, ginger and ½ teaspoon salt.
3. Lightly season the fillets with salt and pepper and place on a baking sheet.
4. Broil for 4 minutes. Brush each fillet with some of the lime-ginger butter and continue to broil for 1 minute or until the fish is done to your liking.

Storing Fish

How to store fresh fish: The best way to store fresh fish is not to store it at all, but rather use it the day you purchase it. If that's not an option, lay the fish on a bed of ice and then cover it. Make sure that the ice has somewhere to drain so that the fish doesn't end up sitting in water, which will cause it to turn mushy.

Quick Asian-Fried Fish

 Serves 2

2 firm-fleshed fish fillets, approximately 1-inch thick

Lemon juice

½ teaspoon salt

½ teaspoon black pepper

½ teaspoon turmeric

1–1½ tablespoon vegetable oil

½ medium onion, thinly sliced

½ clove garlic, chopped

½ (1-inch) piece ginger, peeled and minced

1 serrano chili, seeded and minced

1 tablespoon almond slivers

1 teaspoon cumin

1 teaspoon cardamom

⅛ teaspoon cinnamon

¹⁄₁₆ teaspoon ground clove

1 tablespoon boiling water

¼ cup plain yogurt

This fish gets its flavoring from the unique sauce. The finished fish is packed with flavor, but if you like, a squeeze of lemon or lime juice certainly won't hurt.

1. Rinse the fish with cold water and pat dry. Rub the fish with lemon juice.
2. Combine the salt, pepper, and turmeric; sprinkle over the fish.
3. Heat 1 tablespoon of vegetable oil in a large frying pan over high heat. Brown the fish quickly on each side. Remove the fish to a plate, cover, and set aside.
4. Add the onion to the same pan and sauté until translucent and just beginning to brown.
5. Place the cooked onion in a food processor along with the garlic, ginger, chilies, and almonds. Process to form a paste, adding a bit of water if necessary. Add the cumin, cardamom, cinnamon, and clove; process to thoroughly blend.
6. If necessary, add additional vegetable oil to the frying pan to make about 1½ tablespoons. Heat the oil over medium. Add the spice mixture and cook, stirring constantly, for about 2 minutes. Swirl a bit of water in the food processor to remove any remaining spices and pour it into the pan; stir to combine.
7. Pour the boiling water into the frying pan and stir in the yogurt. Bring to a simmer and let the sauce cook for 5 minutes.
8. Add the fish to the sauce, turning to coat. Cover and let simmer for approximately 10 minutes or until the fish is done to your liking.

CHAPTER 6

PORK AND POULTRY

Pork, Carrot, and Celery Spring Rolls

 Yields 5 rolls

½ tablespoon vegetable oil

¼ teaspoon minced garlic

¼ cup minced or ground pork

½ cup grated carrots

½ cup chopped celery

⅛ cup fish sauce

½ tablespoon sugar

⅛ teaspoon white pepper

¼ cup bean sprouts

5 spring roll wrappers

1 egg yolk, beaten

Vegetable oil for deep frying

Thai recipes often call for ground meat. Make sure to use low-fat meat so that when you combine it with other ingredients, it remains crumbly and doesn't add excess moisture or fat to your dish.

1. In a large skillet, heat the ½ tablespoon of vegetable oil over medium-high heat. Add the garlic and pork, and sauté until the pork is cooked through.
2. Add the carrots, celery, fish sauce, sugar, and white pepper. Increase heat to high and cook for 1 minute.
3. Drain any liquid from the pan and allow the mixture to cool to room temperature, then stir in the bean sprouts.
4. On a clean, dry work surface, place the egg roll wrapper with an end pointing toward you, forming a diamond. Place approximately 2 tablespoons of the filling on the lower portion of the wrapper. Fold up the corner nearest you and roll once, then fold in the sides. Brush the remaining point with the egg yolk and finish rolling to seal. Repeat with the remaining wrappers and filling.
5. Heat 2 to 3 inches of oil to 350°F. Deep-fry the spring rolls until golden brown; remove immediately to drain on paper towels.
6. Serve with sweet-and-sour sauce.

Barbecued Pork on Rice

 Serves 2

Total Cost: $4.63

1 pork tenderloin, trimmed of excess fat

2 tablespoons sugar

2 tablespoons soy sauce

1 teaspoon Chinese 5-spice powder

1 hard-boiled egg, peeled

2 tablespoons flour

1½ cups water

2 tablespoons rice vinegar

1 tablespoon sesame seeds, toasted

Jasmine rice, cooked according to package directions

1 cucumber, thinly sliced

1 green onion, trimmed and thinly sliced

This in not a typical barbecue. Nevertheless, I think you will find yourself asking for more once you've tried this Asian version of what we Americans think of as an indigenous cuisine.

1. Slice the tenderloin into medallions approximately ¼-inch thick. Place the medallions in a mixing bowl.
2. Combine the sugar, soy sauce, and 5-spice powder in a small bowl. Pour the soy mixture over pork strips and toss the strips until thoroughly coated. Let marinate at least 30 minutes, but preferably overnight.
3. Preheat the oven to 350°F. Place the pork pieces in a single layer on a baking sheet lined with foil. Reserve any leftover marinade. Bake the pork for approximately 1 hour. The pork with be firm and rather dry, but not burned. It will also have a reddish color.
4. Place the reserved marinade in a small saucepan and heat to boiling. Turn off the heat and add the peeled egg, rolling it in the sauce to color it. Remove the egg and set it aside. When cool enough to handle, slice it into thin pieces.
5. Combine the flour and water, and add it to the marinade. Bring to a boil to thicken, then remove from heat.
6. Add the vinegar and the sesame seeds. Adjust seasoning by adding additional sugar and/ or soy sauce.
7. To serve, place some Jasmine rice in the center of each plate. Fan a few pieces of the pork around one side of the rice. Fan some cucumber slices and sliced hard-boiled egg around the other side. Spoon some of the sauce over the pork and sprinkle with the green onion slices.

Pork with Garlic and Crushed Black Pepper

Serves 2

$ Total Cost: $4.02

10–20 garlic cloves, mashed

2–2½ teaspoons black peppercorns, coarsely ground

4 tablespoons vegetable oil

1 pork tenderloin, trimmed of all fat and cut into medallions about ¼-inch thick

¼ cup sweet black soy sauce

2 tablespoons brown sugar

2 tablespoons fish sauce

Be sure to use the freshest, highest quality pepper you can find. I like the rich Tellicherry peppercorns from India. Whatever type of pepper you choose, make sure it is freshly ground in order to achieve its maximum flavor potential.

1. Place the garlic and the black pepper in a small food processor and process briefly to form a coarse paste; set aside.
2. Heat the oil in a wok or large skillet over medium-high heat. When the oil is hot, add the garlic-pepper paste and stir-fry until the garlic turns gold.
3. Raise the heat to high and add the pork medallions; stir-fry for 30 seconds.
4. Add the soy sauce and brown sugar, stirring until the sugar is dissolved.
5. Add the fish sauce and continue to cook until the pork is cooked through, about another 1 to 2 minutes.

Pork Medallions in a Clay Pot

 Serves 2

1 tablespoon oyster sauce

1 tablespoon light soy sauce

1 tablespoon sweet (dark) soy sauce

½ tablespoon black bean paste

½ teaspoon sesame oil

½ teaspoon rice wine

¼ teaspoon ground black pepper

½ clove garlic, minced

½ tablespoon cornstarch

1 pork tenderloins, trimmed and cut into ½-inch slices

1 tablespoon vegetable oil

½ tablespoon tamarind concentrate

½ cup water

Soy sauce, black bean paste, sesame oil, and rice wine are all traditional Chinese ingredients. The Chinese use clay pots over an open heat source as a type of oven, an appliance still not used much in Asia.

1. Prepare the marinade by combining the oyster sauce, light and dark soy sauces, black bean paste, sesame oil, rice wine, black pepper, garlic, and cornstarch in a medium bowl.
2. Add the pork slices to the bowl of marinade and toss to coat thoroughly. Cover the pork and let marinate at room temperature for 30 minutes.
3. Heat the vegetable oil in a wok over medium-high heat. Add the marinated pork and stir-fry for 3 to 4 minutes.
4. Transfer the pork to a clay pot or other ovenproof braising vessel.
5. Stir together the tamarind and water; pour over the pork.
6. Bake the pork in a 350°F oven for 1½ hours, until very tender.

Pork and Spinach Curry

 Serves 1–2

¾ cup coconut milk, divided

1 tablespoon red curry paste

½ cup lean pork strips

2 cups water

½ lime

2 kaffir lime leaves, crumbled

3½ tablespoons fish sauce

2 tablespoons sugar

½ pound baby spinach

Rice, cooked according to package directions

Some meat departments actually offer meats precut into strips, which dramatically reduces prep time. If pork strips are not available, try this recipe with beef, chicken, or turkey. To make it super healthy, use light coconut milk.

1. In a medium-sized saucepan, heat ½ cup of the coconut milk and the curry paste over medium-low heat, stirring to combine thoroughly. Cook for 5 minutes, stirring constantly, so that the sauce does not burn.
2. Add the pork cubes, the remaining coconut milk, and the water. Return the mixture to a simmer and let cook for 5 minutes. Squeeze the juice of the lime half into the curry. Add the lime half.
3. Stir in the kaffir lime leaves, fish sauce, and sugar. Continue simmering for 5 to 10 more minutes or until the pork is cooked through. Remove the lime half.
4. Add the baby spinach and cook for 1 minute.
5. Serve over rice.

Sweet-and-Sour Chicken

 Serves 2

1 tablespoon soy sauce

1 clove garlic, minced

½ (1-inch) piece of ginger, peeled and minced

½–1 tablespoon prepared chili sauce

6 ounces boneless, skinless chicken breasts, cut into 1-inch cubes

½ tablespoon vegetable oil

½ small onion, thinly sliced

½ green and ½ red bell pepper, seeded and cut into 1-inch pieces

4 ounces canned pineapple pieces, drained

2–3 tablespoon prepared Plum Sauce (see recipe to follow)

Jasmine rice, cooked according to package directions

A classic Asian dish that we have all tried at one time or another. The green and red peppers complement the sweetness of the pineapple. The chili sauce offsets the plum sauce. And the whole thing is great!

1. In a small bowl, combine the soy sauce, garlic, ginger, and chili sauce. Add the chicken pieces, stirring to coat. Set aside to marinate for at least 20 minutes.
2. Heat the oil in a wok or large skillet over medium heat. Add the onion and sauté until translucent, about 3 minutes.
3. Add the chicken mixture and continue to cook for another 3 to 5 minutes.
4. Add the bell peppers, the pineapple, and plum sauce. Cook for an additional 5 minutes or until the chicken it cooked through.
5. Serve over lots of fluffy Jasmine rice.

PLUM SAUCE

 Yields ⅔ cup

1 12-ounce can prune plums, drained

2 tablespoons brown sugar

4 tablespoons rice vinegar

1 slice ginger

1 clove garlic

½ cup canned juice from the drained plums

½ cup water

For best results, prepare the plum sauce several hours ahead of time to give the flavors a chance to blend.

1. Remove the plum pits. In a medium saucepan, bring all the ingredients to a boil. Simmer, covered, for about 2 hours, or until the plums are soft.
2. Remove the ginger and garlic. Process the sauce in a blender or food processor until smooth. Cool and chill in the refrigerator. Use within a few days.

Thai-Style Green Curry Chicken

 Serves 2

⅛ cup vegetable oil

1½ whole boneless, skinless chicken breasts, cut into bite-sized pieces

⅛ cup green curry paste

1 cup coconut milk

1¼ tablespoon fish sauce

⅛ cup (or to taste) chopped cilantro leaves

Steamed white rice

Vegetables can easily be added to this dish if you like: Stir in snow peas 5 minutes before the curry is done cooking and a handful of baby spinach leaves just at the last moment.

1. Heat 2 tablespoons of vegetable oil in a large sauté pan or wok over medium heat. Add the chicken and sauté until lightly browned on all sizes. Remove the chicken and set aside.
2. Add the remaining vegetable oil to the sauté pan. Stir in the curry paste and cook for 2 to 3 minutes. Add the coconut milk and continue to cook for 5 minutes. Add the reserved chicken and fish sauce. Reduce heat and simmer until chicken is tender, 15 to 20 minutes. Stir in the cilantro.
3. Serve with steamed white rice.

Reducing Chili Fire
Roasting chilies is another way to tone down their heat, as is soaking them in ice water for an hour.

Lemongrass Chicken Skewers

 Serves 2

2½ stalks lemongrass, trimmed

4 large cubes chicken breast meat, a little over 1 ounce each

Black pepper

1 tablespoon vegetable oil, divided

Pinch of dried red pepper flakes

Juice of 1 lime

1 teaspoon fish sauce

Pinch of sugar

Sea salt to taste

These chicken skewers are based on a recipe from award-winning chef Jean-Georges Vongerichten, whose French-inspired Thai cuisine has won praise the world over. Vongerichten has a line of tasty sauces and marinades that is available in stores.

1. Remove 2 inches from the thick end of each stalk of lemongrass; set aside. Bruise ½ of the lemongrass stalks with the back of a knife. Remove the tough outer layer of the fifth stalk, exposing the tender core; mince.
2. Skewer 2 cubes of chicken on each lemongrass stalk. Sprinkle the skewers with the minced lemongrass and black pepper, and drizzle with 1 tablespoon of oil. Cover with plastic wrap and refrigerate for 12 to 24 hours.
3. Chop all of the reserved lemongrass stalk ends. Place in a small saucepan and cover with water. Bring to a boil, cover, and let reduce until approximately 2 tablespoons of liquid is left; strain. Return the liquid to the saucepan and further reduce to 1 tablespoon.
4. Combine the lemongrass liquid with the red pepper flakes, lime juice, fish sauce, sugar, and remaining tablespoon of oil; set aside.
5. Prepare a grill to high heat. Grill the chicken skewers for approximately 2 to 3 minutes per side, or until done to your liking.
6. To serve, spoon a little of the lemongrass sauce over the top of each skewer and sprinkle with sea salt.

Tamarind Stir-Fried Chicken with Mushrooms

 Serves 1–2

2 tablespoons vegetable oil

1–2 whole boneless, skinless chicken breasts, cut into bite-sized cubes

Salt and freshly ground black pepper

1 teaspoon sugar

4 ounces domestic mushrooms, sliced

½ cup sliced onions

1 clove garlic, minced

2 tablespoons tamarind concentrate

2 tablespoons water

1 cup bean sprouts

1 small jalapeño, seeded and minced

¼ cup chopped basil

This recipe calls for domestic mushrooms and it's great as is. But don't hesitate to experiment—try portobellos, creminis, shiitakes, or—if you want a special treat—morels. Just cut them into bite-sized pieces and go for it!

1. Heat the vegetable oil in a large sauté pan or wok over high heat. Season the chicken with the salt, pepper, and sugar.
2. Add the chicken to the pan and stir-fry for 2 minutes. Add the mushrooms, onions, and garlic; continue to cook for an additional 2 to 3 minutes. Add the tamarind and water; stir.
3. Add the remaining ingredients. Adjust seasonings to taste and serve.

Thai Cashew Chicken

Serves 2

3 tablespoons vegetable oil

5–10 dried Thai chilies

5–10 cloves garlic, mashed

1 large whole boneless, skin-less chicken breast, cut into thin strips

3 green onions, trimmed and cut into 1-inch lengths

1 small onion, thinly sliced

2–3 teaspoons Chili Tamarind Paste (see recipe to follow)

¼ cup chicken broth

1 tablespoon oyster sauce

1 tablespoon fish sauce

2 tablespoons sugar

½ cup whole cashews

This is a rather pungent curry. To tone it down, reduce the number of chilies and garlic, and warn guests not to eat the dried chilies.

1. In a wok or large skillet, heat the oil over medium-high heat until hot.
2. Add the chilies and stir-fry briefly until they darken in color. Transfer the chilies to a paper towel to drain; set aside.
3. Add the garlic to the wok and stir-fry until just beginning to turn golden.
4. Raise the heat to high and add the chicken. Cook, stirring constantly, for approximately 1 minute.
5. Add the green onions and onion slices and cook for 30 seconds.
6. Add the Chili Tamarind Paste, broth, oyster sauce, fish sauce, and sugar. Continue to stir-fry for 30 more seconds.
7. Add the reserved chilies and the cashews; stir-fry for 1 more minute or until the chicken is cooked through and the onions are tender.

Chili Nutrition

Fresh chilies are rich in vitamins A, C, and E. Red chilies (i.e., ripe) have the most nutritional value. Cooking chilies lessens their vitamin levels and drying them destroys most of their vitamins.

The $5 Takeout Cookbook

CHILI TAMARIND PASTE

 Yields approximately 3 cups

½ cup dried shrimp

1¾ cups vegetable oil, divided

⅓ cup garlic

1 cup sliced shallot

12 small Thai chilies or 6 serrano chilies

3 tablespoon tamarind concentrate

3 tablespoons brown sugar

1 tablespoon fish sauce

1. Place the dried shrimp in a small bowl. Cover the shrimp with water, stir briefly, and drain; set aside.
2. Pour 1½ cups of the vegetable oil in a medium-sized saucepan. Bring the oil to approximately 360°F over medium-high heat.
3. Add the garlic and fry until golden brown. Using a slotted spoon, transfer the garlic to a bowl lined with paper towels.
4. Add the shallots to the saucepan and fry for 2 to 3 minutes; transfer the shallots to the bowl with the garlic.
5. Fry the reserved shrimp in the saucepan for 2 minutes; transfer to the bowl.
6. Fry the chilies until they become brittle, about 30 seconds; transfer them to the bowl. (Allow oil to cool to room temperature before discarding.)
7. Combine the fried ingredients, the remaining oil, and the tamarind in a food processor; process to form a smooth paste.
8. Place the paste in a small saucepan over medium heat. Add the sugar and fish sauce, and cook, stirring occasionally, for about 5 minutes.
9. Allow the paste to return to room temperature before placing in an airtight container.

Thai Glazed Chicken

 Serves 2

1 whole chicken, cut in half (ask your butcher to do this for you)

1 teaspoon salt

4 cloves garlic, chopped

1 teaspoon white pepper

1 tablespoon minced cilantro

2 tablespoons rice wine

2 tablespoons coconut milk

1 tablespoon fish sauce

1 teaspoon chopped ginger

2 tablespoons soy sauce

The marinade for this dish looks rather like watered-down milk, but don't let the blah appearance fool you: It's delicious. Unlike many Thai marinades, this one is not terribly spicy. The only heat comes from the pepper and ginger.

1. Rinse the chicken under cold water, then pat dry. Trim off any excess fat or skin. Place the chicken halves in large Ziploc bags.
2. Stir the remaining ingredients together in a small bowl until well combined.
3. Pour the marinade into the Ziploc bags, seal closed, and turn until the chicken is evenly coated with the marinade. Let the chicken marinate for 30 minutes to 1 hour in the refrigerator.
4. Preheat the oven to 350°F.
5. Remove the chicken from the bags and place them breast side up in a roasting pan large enough to hold them comfortably. (Discard the remaining marinade.)
6. Roast the chicken for 45 minutes.
7. Turn on the broiler and broil for approximately 10 minutes or until done.

Siamese Roast Chicken

 Serves 2

2 stalks lemongrass, thinly sliced (tender inner core only)

1 medium onion, chopped

1 clove garlic, minced

1 teaspoon (or to taste) dried red pepper flakes

1 tablespoon fish sauce

1 whole roasting chicken

Salt and pepper to taste

Vegetable oil

1. To prepare the marinade, place the lemongrass, onion, garlic, red pepper, and fish sauce in a food processor. Process until a thick paste is formed. Refrigerate for at least 30 minutes, overnight if possible.
2. Spread the marinade throughout the chicken cavity and then sprinkle the cavity with salt and pepper. Rub the outside of the bird with a bit of vegetable oil (or butter if you prefer) and season with salt and pepper. Place the bird in a roasting pan, and cover it with plastic wrap. Refrigerate for a few hours to marinate, if possible. Remove the chicken from the refrigerator approximately 30 minutes before roasting.
3. Preheat the oven to 500°F. Remove the plastic wrap and place the bird in the oven, legs first, and roast for 50 to 60 minutes or until the juices run clear.

Using Pan Drippings

Pan drippings from any roasted poultry or meat make a great "sauce" for pouring over potatoes or noodles. After you have removed the roast from the pan, pour off any fat. Place the roasting pan on a burner over medium-high heat. Add approximately ½ cup of liquid—water, stock, wine—and bring to a boil. Scrape up the browned bits off the bottom of the roaster. Cook until the liquid is reduced by about half. Remove from heat and check seasonings; adjust if necessary.

Ginger Chicken

Serves 2

½ tablespoon fish sauce

½ tablespoon dark soy sauce

½ tablespoon oyster sauce

3 tablespoons vegetable oil

1 tablespoon chopped garlic

1 whole boneless, skinless chicken breast, cut into bite-sized pieces

¾ cup sliced domestic mushrooms

1 tablespoon grated ginger

Pinch of sugar

3 tablespoons chopped onion

Jasmine rice, cooked according to package directions

1 green onion, trimmed and cut into 1-inch pieces

Cilantro

Ginger is one of the most well-known of all of the Asian flavoring agents. Its bright, clean, slightly sweet, slightly hot flavor is found in everything from savory stir-fries like this one to desserts to beverages.

1. In a small bowl combine the fish, soy, and oyster sauces; set aside.
2. Heat the oil in a large wok until very hot. Add the garlic and chicken, and stir fry just until the chicken begins to change color.
3. Add the reserved sauce and cook until it begins to simmer, stirring constantly.
4. Add the mushrooms, ginger, sugar, onion, and chilies; simmer until the chicken is cooked through, about 8 minutes.
5. To serve, ladle the chicken over Jasmine rice and top with green onion and cilantro.

Poultry Protection

Be careful with raw poultry. It often contains bacteria that can cause food-born illness. Keep it refrigerated at all times, even when thawing it, in a leak-proof container. Thoroughly clean all utensils and cutting boards. Sanitize them in a dishwasher or with a bleach solution. Thoroughly wash your hands with hot water and soup after handling raw poultry.

Tandoori Chicken

 Serves 2

2 skinless chicken breasts

2 skinless chicken legs

¼ cup plain yogurt

½ tablespoon grated ginger

1 small garlic cloves, minced

1 teaspoon salt

¹⁄₁₆ teaspoon chili powder

1 teaspoon paprika

¾ teaspoon Garam Masala
    (see recipe to follow)

1 tablespoon ghee, melted

Without a tandoori oven, you can't really make an authentic tandoori dish. The clay used in making the ovens gives a smoky flavor that can't be achieved any other way. Still, this recipe creates an acceptable variation.

1. Using a small, sharp knife, make 3 to 4 (¼-inch-deep) slits in each piece of chicken. Set aside in a bowl large enough to hold all of the pieces.
2. Grind together the ginger, garlic, salt, chili pepper, paprika, and garam masala. Stir the spice mixture into the yogurt.
3. Pour the yogurt over the chicken, making sure that all of the pieces are coated. Cover and marinate overnight, turning the pieces in the marinade every so often.
4. Preheat the oven to 450°F.
5. Add the ghee to a roasting pan large enough to hold all of the chicken pieces. Add the chicken, breast side down. Spoon some of the ghee over the pieces. Roast for 10 minutes. Turn the pieces over, baste again, and continue roasting for 5 minutes. Turn them again and roast for an additional 5 minutes. Turn 1 last time (breasts should be up); baste and cook until done, about 5 more minutes.

GARAM MASALA

 Makes approximately ⅓ cup

$ Total Cost: $3.63

4 tablespoons coriander seeds

2 tablespoons cumin seeds

1 tablespoon whole black peppercorns

2 teaspoons cardamom seeds

2 small cinnamon sticks, broken into pieces

1 teaspoon whole cloves

The Indian spice mix you can't do without! If you always have a bit of this mixture on hand, you are just a step away from great Indian cuisine. I promise. (Garam masala is also available in specialty stores.)

1. In a small heavy sauté pan, individually dry roast each spice over medium-high heat until they begin to release their aroma.
2. Allow the spices to cool to room temperature and then place them in a spice grinder and process to form a fairly fine powder.
3. Store in an airtight container.

Cambodian-Style Pan-Fried Chicken and Mushrooms

 Serves 2

3 ounces fresh mushrooms

1 tablespoon vegetable oil

2 cloves garlic, crushed

¼ teaspoon grated ginger

¾ pound chicken breasts and legs

½ cup water

1 teaspoon sugar

This dish reminds me of my mom's moist and delicious pan-fried chicken, except hers didn't have garlic or ginger. Spoon the seasoned mushrooms and a bit of the pan drippings over the chicken. Serve noodles on the side.

1. Rinse mushrooms under cold water; drain again and squeeze dry. Remove any tough stems. Cut the mushrooms into bite-sized pieces; set aside.
2. Place the vegetable oil in a wok or large skillet over medium-high heat. Add the garlic and the ginger and stir-fry briefly.
3. Add the chicken and fry until the skin turns golden.
4. Stir in the water and the sugar. Add the mushrooms.
5. Reduce the heat to low, cover, and cook until the chicken is tender, about 30 minutes.

Honeyed Chicken

 Serves 1–2

1 tablespoon honey

1 tablespoon fish sauce

1 tablespoon soy sauce

¼ teaspoon Chinese 5-spice powder

1 tablespoon vegetable oil

½ medium onion, peeled and cut into wedges

½ pound boneless, skinless chicken breasts, cut into bite-sized pieces

1–2 cloves garlic, thinly sliced

½ (1-inch) piece ginger, peeled and minced

This is a version of a sweet-and-sour chicken without the bell peppers, fried batter, or red food coloring! The glaze is multidimensional in its flavor profile so the peppers aren't missed, and no batter means a healthier dish.

1. Combine the honey, fish sauce, soy sauce, and 5-spice powder in a small bowl; set aside.
2. Heat the oil in a wok on medium-high. Add the onion and cook until it just begins to brown.
3. Add the chicken; stir-fry for 3 to 4 minutes.
4. Add the garlic and ginger, and continue stir-frying for 30 more seconds.
5. Stir in the honey mixture and let cook for 3 to 4 minutes, until the chicken is glazed and done to your liking.

Chili-Fried Chicken

 Serves 2

1½ tablespoon tamarind concentrate

Pinch of turmeric

¼ teaspoon ground coriander

¾ teaspoon salt, divided

¼ teaspoon white pepper

1½ pounds chicken pieces, rinsed and patted dry

1 tablespoon vegetable oil

3 large red chilies, seeded and chopped

1 small onions, thinly sliced

Vegetable oil for deep-frying

Like the colonel's version, this fried chicken is good hot, at room temperature, or cold.

1. In a small bowl combine the tamarind, turmeric, coriander, 1 teaspoon of the salt, and the pepper.
2. Place the chicken pieces in a large Ziploc bag. Pour the tamarind mixture over the chicken, seal the bag, and marinate at least 2 hours or overnight in the refrigerator.
3. In a small sauté pan, heat 2 tablespoons of vegetable oil over medium heat. Add the red chilies, onions, and the remaining salt; sauté for 5 minutes. Set aside to cool slightly.
4. Transfer the chili mixture to a food processor and pulse briefly to form a coarse sauce.
5. Drain the chicken and discard the marinade. Deep-fry the chicken pieces in hot oil until the skin is golden and the bones are crispy. Remove the cooked chicken to paper towels to drain.
6. Place the cooked chicken in a large mixing bowl. Pour the chili sauce over the chicken and toss until each piece is evenly coated.

Jungle Chicken

Serves 3

2–4 serrano chilies, stems and seeds removed

1 stalk lemongrass, inner portion roughly chopped

2 (2-inch-long, ½-inch-wide) strips of lime peel

2 tablespoons vegetable oil

½ cup coconut milk

1 whole boneless, skinless chicken breast, cut into thin strips

2–4 tablespoons fish sauce

10–15 basil leaves

This is a typical recipe from the north of Thailand, which is covered with dense jungle and is home to a variety of endangered species, most notably the tiger. Like the tiger, this dish can be a bit ferocious and can pack quite a bite! So beware!

1. Place the chilies, lemongrass, and lime peel into a food processor and process until ground.
2. Heat the oil over medium-high heat in a wok or large skillet. Add the chili mixture and sauté for 1 to 2 minutes.
3. Stir in the coconut milk and cook for 2 minutes.
4. Add the chicken and cook until the chicken is cooked through, about 5 minutes.
5. Reduce heat to low and add the fish sauce and basil leaves to taste.
6. Serve with plenty of Jasmine rice.

CHAPTER 7

VEGETABLE DISHES

Vegetables Poached in Coconut Milk

 Serves 2–4

1 cup coconut milk

1 shallot, finely chopped

1 tablespoon soy sauce

1 tablespoon brown sugar

1 tablespoon Thai chilies, seeded and finely sliced

1 tablespoon green peppercorns, tied together in a small pouch made from a Handi Wipe

½ teaspoon sliced kaffir lime leaves

½ cup long beans or green beans, broken into 2-inch pieces

½ cup sliced mushrooms

1 cup shredded cabbage

½ cup peas

Rice, cooked according to package directions

Each vegetable in this dish is rather mild in flavor and tends to absorb different amounts of the poaching liquid, giving the diner a slightly different flavor sensation with every bite. If you can't find kaffir limes, regular limes make an acceptable substitute.

1. In a saucepan bring the coconut milk to a gentle simmer over medium heat. Stir in the shallots, soy sauce, brown sugar, chilies, green peppercorn pouch, and lime leaves. Simmer for 1 to 2 minutes until aromatic.
2. Add the green beans, mushrooms, and cabbage, and return to a simmer. Cook for 5 to 10 minutes or until tender.
3. Add the peas and cook 1 more minute. Remove the pouch of peppercorns before serving over rice.

Thai-Style Bean Sprouts and Snap Peas

 Serves 2

1 tablespoon vegetable oil

½ small onion, thinly sliced

½ (1-inch) piece ginger, peeled and minced

Pinch of white pepper

½ tablespoon soy sauce

¼ pound sugar snap peas, trimmed

½ pound bean sprouts, rinsed thoroughly and trimmed if necessary

Salt and sugar to taste

This recipe lets the peas shine without overpowering their sweet, delicate flavor with anything heavy or overly spicy. The bean sprouts add a nice contrast.

1. Heat the vegetable oil over medium-high heat in a large skillet.
2. Add the onion and the ginger and sauté for 1 minute.
3. Stir in the white pepper and the soy sauce.
4. Add the sugar snap peas and cook, stirring constantly, for 1 minute.
5. Add the bean sprouts and cook for 1 more minutes while stirring constantly.
6. Add up to ½ teaspoon of salt and a large pinch of sugar to adjust the balance of the sauce. Serve immediately.

Stir-Fried Black Mushrooms and Asparagus

 Serves 2

 Total Cost: $3.16

½ ounce dried Chinese black mushrooms

½ tablespoon vegetable oil

½–1 cloves garlic, minced

1½–2 tablespoons oyster sauce

Tabasco (optional)

½ pound asparagus spears, trimmed

The unique sauce in this dish is a far cry from the traditional, super-rich Hollandaise sauce or butter and nutmeg traditionally served with asparagus in the West.

1. Place the dried mushrooms in a bowl and cover with hot water. Let soak for 15 minutes. Drain, discard the stems, and slice into strips; set aside.
2. Heat the oil on medium-high in a large skillet. Add the garlic and sauté until golden.
3. Stir in the mushrooms and continue cooking, stirring constantly, for 1 minute.
4. Stir in the oyster sauce and a few drops of Tabasco if desired.
5. Add the asparagus spears. Sauté for 2 to 4 minutes or until the asparagus is done to your liking.

Thai Vegetable Curry

 Serves 2

1 tablespoon vegetable oil

⅛ cup green curry paste

1 cup canned, unsweetened coconut milk

1 tablespoon fish sauce

½ pound small boiling potatoes, quartered (or halved if large)

⅓ pound Japanese eggplant, cut into 1-inch slices

6 ounces baby carrots

1 cup broccoli florets

1½–2 ounces green beans, cut into 1-inch lengths

¼ cup fresh minced cilantro

Don't be afraid to be an experimental cook, especially with vegetables. In this recipe you can add just about any veggies you want. Try substituting sweet potatoes for the boiling potatoes and Brussels sprouts for the broccoli.

1. In a heavy stew pot, heat the oil. Add the curry paste and cook for 2 to 3 minutes.
2. Add the coconut milk and fish sauce; simmer for 5 minutes.
3. Add the potatoes, eggplant, and carrots, and bring to a boil. Reduce heat and simmer for 10 minutes. Add the broccoli and green beans; continue to simmer until the vegetables are cooked through, about 10 minutes.
4. Just before serving stir in the cilantro.

Soy Sauce?

The Thai will know immediately that you are a foreigner if you ask for soy sauce. It's usually available, but it is not a traditional condiment. Fish sauce is the way to go.

Southeastern Vegetable Stew

Serves 2

2 cups vegetable stock

¾ tablespoons fish sauce

½ tablespoon dark soy sauce

½ tablespoon brown sugar

½ cup turnip, cut into bite-sized pieces

¼ Chinese cabbage, cut into bite-sized pieces

¼ cup sliced leeks

¼ can straw mushrooms, drained

¼ teaspoon vegetable oil

1½ tablespoon soybean paste

¾ tablespoons chopped garlic

¼ tablespoon minced ginger

½ cup bean noodles, soaked, and cut into short lengths

⅛ cup chopped cilantro

Freshly ground pepper to taste

1. Bring the stock to a boil and add the fish sauce, soy sauce, and brown sugar.
2. Reduce the heat, add the vegetables, and simmer until the vegetables are almost tender.
3. In a small sauté pan, heat the oil over medium heat. Add the soybean paste and stir-fry until fragrant. Add the garlic and ginger, and stir-fry until the garlic is golden.
4. Add the soybean paste mixture to the soup. Stir in the noodles and cilantro, and simmer 5 more minutes.
5. Season with the pepper and additional fish sauce to taste.

The $5 Takeout Cookbook

Asian Grilled Vegetables

 Serves 3

1 bell pepper (red, yellow, or green, in any combination), seeded and cut into 2-inch squares

½ zucchini, cut into 1-inch slices

½ summer squash, cut into 1-inch slices

6 whole mushrooms, approximately 1-inch in diameter

6 whole pearl onions or 12 (2-inch) pieces of white onion

½ recipe Asian Marinade (see recipe to follow)

If you are planning on serving your vegetables from a bowl, don't bother with the skewers. Simply place the vegetables in a pan, marinate them, and then place them in a grill basket to cook.

1. Alternate the vegetables on 6 skewers (soak the skewers in water until soft if using wooden skewers.)
2. Place the skewers in a pan large enough to allow them to lay flat. Pour the marinade over the skewers and let set for approximately 1 hour.
3. Place the skewers in a lightly oiled grill basket and place on a hot grill. Cook approximately 5 minutes on each side or until vegetables are done to your liking.

ASIAN MARINADE

 Yields approximately 1¼ cups

 Total Cost: $3.85

¼ cup fish sauce

¼ cup soy sauce (preferably low-sodium)

½ cup freshly squeezed lime juice

2 tablespoons crunchy peanut butter

1 tablespoon light brown sugar

1 tablespoon curry powder

1 teaspoon minced garlic

Crushed dried red pepper

Combine all the ingredients in a blender or food processor and blend until smooth.

The $5 Takeout Cookbook

Vegetarian Stir-Fry

 Serves 2

½–1 tablespoon vegetable oil

¾ cup bite-sized tofu pieces

1 tablespoon minced garlic

1 tablespoon grated ginger

2 tablespoons seeded and sliced Thai chilies

2 tablespoons soy sauce

1 tablespoon dark sweet soy sauce

½ small onion, sliced

⅛ cup snow peas

⅛ cup thinly sliced celery

⅛ cup water chestnuts

⅛ cup bite-sized pieces bell pepper

⅛ cup sliced mushrooms

⅛ cup cauliflower florets

⅛ cup broccoli florets

⅛ cup asparagus tips

½ tablespoon cornstarch, dissolved in a little water

⅛ cup bean sprouts

Rice, cooked according to package directions

If your vegetable bin ends up looking like mine, with a bit of this and a bit of that, this is the recipe for you. You can follow the ingredient list precisely, or substitute to your hearts desire.

1. Heat 1 tablespoon of oil in a large skillet or wok over medium-high heat. Add the tofu and sauté until golden brown. Transfer the tofu to paper towels to drain.
2. Add additional oil to the skillet if necessary, and stir-fry the garlic, ginger, and chilies to release their fragrance, about 2 to 3 minutes. Stir in the soy sauces and increase the heat to high.
3. Add the reserved tofu and all the vegetables except the bean sprouts; stir-fry for 1 minute.
4. Add the cornstarch mixture and stir-fry for another minute or until the vegetables are just cooked through and the sauce has thickened slightly.
5. Add the bean sprouts, stirring briefly to warm them.
6. Serve over rice.

CHAPTER 8

NOODLE AND RICE DISHES

Pad Thai

 Serves 2–4

8 ounces rice noodles

2 tablespoons vegetable oil

5–6 cloves garlic, finely chopped

2 tablespoons chopped shallots

¼ cup fish sauce

¼ cup brown sugar

6–8 teaspoons tamarind concentrate

¼ cup chopped chives

½ cup chopped roasted peanuts

1 medium egg, beaten

1 cup bean sprouts

Garnish:

1 tablespoon lime juice

1 tablespoon tamarind concentrate

1 tablespoon fish sauce

½ cup bean sprouts

½ cup chopped chives

½ cup coarsely ground roasted peanuts

1 lime cut into wedges

Anyone who has ever eaten in a Thai restaurant has probably had this most famous of Thai noodle dishes. The actual sauce has a rather sweet taste offset by the garlic and peanuts.

1. Soak the noodles in water at room temperature for 30 minutes or until soft. Drain and set aside.
2. Heat the vegetable oil in a wok or skillet over medium-high heat. Add the garlic and shallots, and briefly stir-fry until they begin to change color.
3. Add the reserved noodles and all the remaining ingredients except the egg and the bean sprouts, and stir-fry until hot.
4. While constantly stirring, slowly drizzle in the beaten egg.
5. Add the bean sprouts and cook for no more than another 30 seconds.
6. In a small bowl mix together all of the garnish ingredients except the lime wedges.
7. To serve, arrange the Pad Thai on a serving platter. Top with the garnish and surround with lime wedges.

Pan-Fried Noodles

 Serves 2

$ Total Cost: $1.48

½ pound fresh lo mein noodles or angel hair pasta

⅛ cup minced chives

1 tablespoon (or to taste) prepared chili-garlic paste

1½ tablespoon vegetable oil, divided

Salt to taste

People are always amazed when I tell them that the wedge on their plate is noodles! They are crispy on the outside and still noodlelike inside. I like to serve this with anything grilled or roasted.

1. Boil the noodles in a large pot for no more than 2 to 3 minutes. Drain, rinse under cold water, and drain again.
2. Add the chives, chili paste, 1 tablespoon of the oil, and salt to the noodles; toss to coat, and adjust seasonings.
3. In a heavy-bottomed 10-inch skillet, heat the remaining oil over medium-high heat. When it is hot, add the noodle mixture, spreading evenly. Press the noodles into the pan with the back of a spatula. Cook for approximately 2 minutes. Reduce heat and continue to cook until the noodles are nicely browned. Flip the noodles over in 1 piece. Continue cooking until browned, adding additional oil if necessary.
4. To serve, cut the noodles into wedges.

Noodles of Fun

Other Asian noodles include mein, which are Chinese in origin and are similar to Western egg noodles. They are made with wheat flour, water, and egg, and come fresh, dried, or frozen. Japan also has a variety of noodles, including buckwheat Soba, thin wheat Somen, and thicker, rounder Udon, to name a few.

Thai Noodles with Chicken

 Serves 2

For the sauce:

¼ cup peanut butter

¼ cup soy sauce

½ teaspoon minced garlic

1½ tablespoon sesame oil

1½ tablespoon honey

½ teaspoon hot chili oil

⅛ teaspoon white pepper

For the noodles:

½ pound dry flat Asian noodles

½ tablespoon vegetable oil

½ teaspoon sesame oil

¼ teaspoon minced garlic

¼ pound boneless, skinless chicken breast, cut into thin strips

½ large yellow onion, diced

3–4 green onions, trimmed, white portions sliced, green portion julienned

Hot chili oil adds heat, depth of flavor, and a bit of color. If you use it as a condiment, do so sparingly. It packs a punch and, because it is an oil, quickly permeates whatever it's put on.

1. Place all of the sauce ingredients in a blender and process until smooth; set aside.
2. Bring a large pot of water to boil over high heat. Prepare the noodles according to package directions, drain, and stir in the sauce mixture, reserving ¼ cup; set aside.
3. Heat the oils in a large sauté pan over high heat. Add the garlic and sauté briefly.
4. Add the chicken and onion, and sauté for 5 to 6 minutes or until the chicken is cooked through.
5. Add the white portion of the green onion and sauté for 2 more minutes.
6. Add the green parts of the onions and the remaining sauce, stirring until everything is well coated.
7. To serve, place the noodles on a large platter and top with the meat sauté. Pass additional hot chili oil separately.

Sesame Noodles with Veggies

 Serves 4

2 tablespoons vegetable oil

2 cloves garlic, minced

2 cups broccoli, cut into bite-sized pieces

1 red bell pepper, seeded and cut into strips

2 tablespoons water

8 ounces egg noodles

4 ounces tofu, cut into bite-sized cubes

1 tablespoon sesame oil

2–3 tablespoons soy sauce

2–3 tablespoon prepared chili sauce

3 tablespoons sesame seeds

Sesame oil is a standard ingredient in most Asian cuisines but is not as common in Thai cooking. However, here it pairs well with the other ingredients to create a subtle perfumed quality.

1. Heat the oil in a large sauté pan or wok over medium heat. Add the garlic and sauté until golden, approximately 2 minutes.
2. Add the broccoli and red bell pepper, and stir-fry for 2 to 3 minutes. Add the water, cover, and let the vegetables steam until tender, approximately 5 minutes.
3. Bring a large pot of water to boil. Add the noodles and cook until al dente; drain.
4. While the noodles are cooking, add the remaining ingredients to the broccoli mixture. Remove from heat, add the noodles, and toss to combine.

Spicy Egg Noodles with Sliced Pork

 Serves 2

$ Total Cost: $4.92

1 small cabbage, shredded

1 cup bean sprouts

1 package fresh angel hair pasta

½ teaspoon vegetable oil

4 tablespoons minced garlic

1 tablespoons fish sauce

2 tablespoons sugar

3 tablespoons rice vinegar

2 teaspoons ground dried red chili pepper (or to taste)

⅓ pound roasted pork tenderloin, thinly sliced

Freshly ground black pepper to taste

1 scallion, trimmed and thinly sliced

2 teaspoons chopped cilantro

If you have the barbecued pork on hand, this is another fast preparation. If you don't have leftover pork, but still want to make a quick version of this dish, slice some store-bought roast chicken over the top.

1. Bring a large pot of water to a boil over high heat. Add the cabbage and blanch about 30 seconds. Using a slotted spoon, remove the cabbage from the boiling water; set aside.
2. Let the water return to boiling. Add the bean sprouts and blanch for 10 seconds. Using a slotted spoon, remove the sprouts from the water; set aside.
3. Return the water to boiling. Add the fresh angel hair pasta and cook according to package directions. Drain the pasta and place it in a large mixing bowl.
4. In a small sauté pan, heat the vegetable oil over medium heat. Add the garlic and sauté until golden. Remove from heat. Stir in the fish sauce, sugar, rice vinegar, and dried chili pepper.
5. Pour the sauce over the pasta and toss to coat.
6. To serve, divide the cabbage and the bean sprouts into 2 to 4 portions and place in the center of serving plates. Divide the noodles into 2 to 4 portions and place over the cabbage and sprouts. Divide the pork slices over the noodles. Grind black pepper to taste over the noodles and top with the sliced scallions and chopped cilantro.

Rice Stick Noodles with Chicken and Vegetables

Serves 4

NOODLES:

8 ounces rice stick noodles

2 tablespoons vegetable oil

1 tablespoon sweet black soy
   sauce

Rice noodles don't really have a Western equivalent. Silky smooth and a bit chewy, these rather flavorless delights absorb the flavors of the other ingredients, becoming one with the dish.

1. Soak the noodles in warm water for 15 minutes or until soft; drain.
2. Place a wok over medium-high heat and add the vegetable oil. When the oil is hot, add the noodles and stir-fry vigorously until they are heated through, about 45 seconds to 1 minute.
3. Add the soy sauce and continue to stir-fry for 1 more minute.
4. Place the noodles on a serving platter, covered in foil, in a warm oven until ready to serve.

CHICKEN AND VEGETABLES:

2 tablespoons vegetable oil

4 cloves garlic, chopped

1 large whole boneless, skinless chicken breast, cut into bite-sized strips

¼ pound broccoli, chopped

1 small onion, finely sliced

1½ cups sliced Japanese eggplant

½ teaspoon Tabasco

2 tablespoons fish sauce

2 tablespoons Yellow Bean Sauce (see recipe to follow)

3 tablespoons brown sugar

¼ cup chicken broth

1 tablespoon cornstarch mixed with 1 tablespoon water

½ cup bean sprouts

¼–⅓ cup sliced green onions

1 small red bell pepper, seeded and cut into strips

1. Place a wok over medium-high heat and add the vegetable oil. When the oil is hot, add the garlic and stir-fry briefly to release its aroma.
2. Add the chicken and cook until it starts to become opaque.
3. Add the broccoli and stir-fry for 30 seconds.
4. Add the onion and eggplant and stir-fry for 2 minutes.
5. Add the Tabasco, fish sauce, yellow bean sauce, and sugar. Stir-fry for 1 minute.
6. Add the broth, cornstarch mixture, bean sprouts, green onions, and red bell pepper; cook until vegetables are tender-crisp.
7. To serve, ladle the chicken and vegetable mixture over the reserved noodles.

YELLOW BEAN SAUCE

 Yields approximately 1 cup

$ Total Cost: $2.73

2 tablespoons vegetable oil

1 medium to large onion, minced

2 serrano chilies, seeded and chopped

1 (½-inch) piece ginger, peeled and chopped

1 teaspoon ground coriander

4 tablespoons fermented yellow beans (fermented soybeans)

2 tablespoons lime juice

2 tablespoons water

1. In a medium-sized sauté pan, heat the oil over medium heat. Add the onion and chilies, and sauté until the onion becomes translucent. Stir in the ginger and coriander, and continue to cook for 30 seconds.
2. Add the beans, lime juice, and water, and simmer over low heat for 10 minutes.
3. Transfer the mixture to a blender and process until smooth.

Curried Rice Noodles with Egg

 Serves 2

½ teaspoon ground coriander

½ teaspoon ground cumin

1 teaspoon curry powder

1 tablespoon red curry paste

¾ cup coconut milk

2–3 cups water

2 tablespoons minced shallots

2 tablespoon sugar

2 tablespoons fish sauce

½ of a 7-ounce package rice noodles

1 hard-boiled egg, sliced

⅓ cup bean sprouts

1 green onion, trimmed and thinly sliced

2 tablespoons chopped cilantro

The combination of ingredients in this dish create a curry that is a bit spicy but has definite sweet overtones.

1. In a small bowl, thoroughly combine the coriander, cumin, curry powder, and curry paste.
2. Pour the coconut milk into a medium-sized saucepan. Stir in the curry paste mixture and place over medium heat. Bring to a simmer and cook for about 5 minutes or until a thin layer of yellow oil begins to form on the surface of the sauce.
3. Stir in 2 cups of the water, the shallots, sugar, and fish sauce. Return the sauce to a simmer and let cook 30 minutes, stirring occasionally and adding additional water if necessary.
4. Meanwhile, soak the noodles in hot water for 10 minutes or until soft.
5. To serve, mound the noodles into serving bowls. Top the noodles with the sliced egg and bean sprouts. Ladle some of the curry sauce over top. Sprinkle with green onion slices and chopped cilantro.

Poached Chicken Breast with Peanut Sauce and Noodles

 Serves 3

⅓ cup crunchy peanut butter

¾ cup coconut milk

1 tablespoon fish sauce

⅛ cup lime juice

1 teaspoon brown sugar

2 cloves garlic, minced

Salt and pepper to taste

⅛ cup chicken stock

⅛ cup half-and-half

½ pound Chinese egg noodles (mein)

½ tablespoon peanut oil

½ tablespoon sesame oil

2–4 green onions, trimmed and thinly sliced

¾ whole boneless, skinless chicken breasts, halved and poached

½ pound snow peas, trimmed and blanched

Using chicken satay as a starting point, this dish is a bit more upscale. It's a great luncheon or brunch item because its not heavy or overpowering, but still rich in flavor.

1. Combine the peanut butter, coconut milk, fish sauce, lime juice, brown sugar, garlic, salt, and pepper in a small saucepan over low heat. Cook until smooth and thick, stirring frequently.
2. Transfer to a blender and purée.
3. Add the chicken stock and half-and-half, and blend; set aside.
4. Bring a large pot of water to a boil. Add the noodles and cook until al dente. Drain, rinse under cold water, and drain again.
5. Toss the noodles with the peanut and sesame oils.
6. To serve, place some pasta in the middle of each serving plate. Spoon some of the peanut sauce over the pasta. Slice each chicken breast on the diagonal. Transfer 1 sliced breast to the top of each portion of noodles. Spoon some additional peanut sauce over the chicken. Surround the noodles with the snow peas. Garnish with the sliced green onions.

Clear Noodles with Baked Shrimp

Serves 2

1 (7-ounce) package rice noodles

2 cloves garlic, chopped

¼ cup chopped cilantro

15–20 black peppercorns

1 tablespoon vegetable oil

1 medium onion, thinly sliced

1 teaspoon sugar

1 tablespoon soy or fish sauce

Sesame oil to taste

6 large shrimp, shell on, rinsed and patted dry

Traditionally, this Chinese-inspired dish would be baked in a clay pot, making for a spectacular presentation. Nevertheless, the shrimp make a spectacular presentation all on their own, and this dish is quite easy to prepare.

1. Soak the noodles in hot water until soft, about 10 minutes. Drain and set aside.
2. Using a mortar and pestle or a food processor, thoroughly combine the garlic, cilantro, and peppercorns.
3. Add the vegetable oil to a wok or large skillet over low heat. Add the garlic mixture and stir-fry for 1 minute. Add the sliced onion and continue cooking until the onion is tender, then turn off the heat.
4. Add the sugar, soy sauce, and a few drops of sesame oil to the wok; stir to combine. Add the noodles and toss to coat. Pour the noodle mixture into an ovenproof baking dish. Place the whole shrimp on top of the noodles, cover the dish, and bake for 20 minutes in a 400°F oven. Serve immediately.

Thai Table Setting

A traditional Thai table setting includes only a fork and spoon. The fork is used to push the food onto the spoon, not to place food into the mouth. Only a spoon is used for this.

The $5 Takeout Cookbook

Singapore Noodles

 Serves 2–3

2 tablespoons vegetable oil

4 cloves garlic, minced

2 tablespoons minced ginger

2 cups cooked chicken in bite-sized pieces

2 green onions, trimmed and thinly sliced

1–2 teaspoons red pepper flakes

¼ cup oyster sauce

3 tablespoons curry powder

2 teaspoons soy sauce

1 package rice sticks, soaked in hot water until soft and drained

Do you have 5 minutes and some leftover chicken, beef, pork, shrimp, or a combination thereof? If so, this is the meal for you. It's satisfying, it's easy, and it's fool proof!

1. Heat the vegetable oil in a wok or large skillet over medium-high heat. Add the garlic and the ginger. Stir-fry until soft.
2. Add the chicken, green onion, and red pepper flakes to the wok; stir-fry until hot.
3. Stir in the oyster sauce, curry powder, and soy sauce. Add the rice noodles and toss. Serve immediately.

Fried Rice with Pineapple and Shrimp

Serves 3

$ Total Cost: $4.95

1 ripe whole pineapple

4 tablespoons vegetable oil

⅓ cup finely chopped onion

2 garlic cloves, finely minced

6 ounces peeled shrimp, deveined and cut into ½-inch pieces

½ teaspoon turmeric

½ teaspoon curry powder

½ teaspoon shrimp paste

2 cups day-old, cooked jasmine or other long-grained rice

Salt to taste

Sugar to taste

This dish makes a great presentation and the fruit and spices complements the shrimp perfectly. Make some extra—this dish reheats in a microwave perfectly, as do almost all fried rice dishes.

1. Preheat the oven to 350°F.
2. In a wok or heavy sauté pan, heat the oil on medium. Add the onion and garlic, and sauté until the onion is translucent. Using a slotted spoon, remove the onions and garlic from the wok and set aside.
3. Add the shrimp and sauté approximately 1 minute; remove and set a side.
4. Add the turmeric, curry powder, and shrimp paste to the wok; stir-fry briefly. Add the rice and stir-fry for 2 to 3 minutes. Add the pineapple and continue to cook. Add the reserved shrimp, onions, and garlic. Season to taste with salt and sugar.
5. Mound the fried rice into a serving bowl and bake for approximately 10 minutes. Serve immediately.

The $5 Takeout Cookbook

Chicken Fried Rice

 Serves 2

½ tablespoon vegetable oil

½ tablespoon minced garlic

½ tablespoon minced ginger

½ medium onion, sliced

¼ medium head Chinese cabbage, coarsely chopped

1½ cup cooked long-grain white rice

⅛ cup fish sauce

⅛ cup dry sherry

⅛ cup chicken stock

½ cup snow peas, trimmed and cut into bite-sized pieces

½ cup shredded, cooked chicken

1 eggs, beaten

Chicken and rice, comfort foods the world over, are combined here in a great tasting entrée. Cabbage and snow peas give the dish a little crunch and the aromatic garlic, ginger, and onion embolden the flavor.

1. In a large skillet or wok, heat the oil over medium-low heat. Add the garlic, ginger, and onion, and stir-fry for 5 minutes or until the onion becomes translucent.
2. Add the cabbage, increase the heat to medium, and stir-fry for 10 minutes.
3. Add the rice and stir-fry for 2 minutes.
4. Combine the fish sauce, sherry, and stock in a small bowl; add to the wok and stir to combine.
5. Add the snow peas and chicken; stir-fry for 2 minutes more.
6. Move the rice to the sides of the wok, forming a hole in the middle. Pour the eggs into the hole and cook for about 1 minute, stirring the eggs with a fork. Fold the cooked eggs into the fried rice.

Serving Rice

In Southeast Asia, baskets are lined with banana leaves or lettuce and used as serving dishes for rice.

PART THREE
PIZZA

With $32 billion worth consumed each year, pizza may just the most popular takeout meal. And it makes sense why—who doesn't enjoy good bread, aromatic and dense, topped with pure oils and the best fruits of earth and sea?

However, making the same, mouth-watering pizza at home isn't hard to do. The trickiest part of making home-made pizza is working with yeast-risen dough; but with a little practice, that can be mastered. In the meantime, if you want to start your home pizza tradition using store-bought dough or ready-to-top bread crust, we promise no one will complain. The scent of warm bread and bubbling cheese from the kitchen will seduce even the toughest pizza snobs.

With this book as your guide, explore the vast world of pizza and pizza-inspired dishes. When you finally pull out a fragrant, cheesy pizza from the oven you'll wonder why you ever called for delivery.

CHAPTER 9

CHEESE AND VEGETABLE

Classic Cheese Pizza

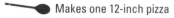 Makes one 12-inch pizza

1 recipe Classic Crust dough (see recipe to follow)

1 tablespoon cornmeal or 1 tablespoon olive oil

¾ cup tomato sauce

½ cup shredded Parmesan cheese

1½ cup shredded mozzarella cheese

Coarsely grate mozzarella and Parmesan cheese just before topping pizza for best flavor.

1. Roll or press pizza dough into 12-inch circle, slightly thicker at the edges than in the center. If using pizza pan, sprinkle the bottom with cornmeal or coat with olive oil and place dough in pan. If using a pizza stone, sprinkle with cornmeal and place stone in oven. Preheat oven to 400°F.
2. Spread ¾ cup sauce in the center of pizza, leaving at least an inch around the edges bare.
3. Sprinkle mozzarella evenly over pizza, just covering the sauce.
4. If using a hot stone or tiles, use a well-floured pizza peel to carefully lift one pizza from preparation surface and place on stone. Bake for 15 to 20 minutes or until the crust is lightly browned and cheese is melted.
5. Remove pizza from oven carefully (use peel if baking with a stone). Set aside to rest briefly before slicing.

CLASSIC CRUST

 Makes crust for one 12-inch pizza

½ package active dry yeast

⅜ cup warm water, about 110°F

¼ teaspoon sugar

⅜ teaspoon salt

1½ cup bread flour

½ tablespoon olive oil

1. In a large measuring cup, dissolve yeast in water. Let stand 5 minutes or until bubbly. Combine sugar, salt, and bread flour in the bowl of a mixer with a dough hook. Or, to mix by hand, place in a large bowl. Make a well in the flour mixture and pour in the water, followed by 1 tablespoon of oil.

2. Turn the mixer on low to blend, or begin stirring the flour into the liquid with a wooden spoon, a little at a time. When ingredients are well combined, turn the mixer on medium-low to knead for 5 minutes. If working dough by hand, turn the dough onto a well-floured work surface. Use a pressing motion with the heels of your hands to push and stretch the dough. Work dough until the mixture is slightly shiny and not too sticky to the touch.

3. The kneaded dough should be divided into four equal pieces. Store any dough not being used in a resealable bag in the refrigerator. Oil remaining dough and place in a bowl, covered, to rise for 1 hour. Punch the dough down, shape into 2 disks, and let rest for 30 minutes.

4. Grab dough by the edges, turning the disk a few inches at a time, allowing gravity to stretch the dough without tearing. Roll the dough into a crust shape or press into a pizza pan. Top as directed in recipe.

Dough for Tomorrow

Pizza dough will rise, albeit slowly, in the refrigerator. To use dough that's been refrigerated overnight, place in a covered bowl on the counter. Punch dough down, then let stand until dough reaches room temperature. Use as directed.

The $5 Takeout Cookbook

Fire-Baked Six-Cheese Pizza

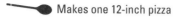

Makes one 12-inch pizza

$ Total Cost: $4.61

1 recipe Classic Crust dough (Chapter 9)

1 tablespoon cornmeal or 1 tablespoon olive oil

¾ cup tomato sauce

¼ cup shredded mozzarella cheese

¼ cup shredded provolone cheese

¼ cup shredded Asiago cheese

¼ cup shredded Parmesan cheese

¼ cup shredded Romano cheese

¼ cup shredded white Cheddar cheese

Like a stronger Asiago flavor? More smoky provolone? Go ahead and change the proportions of these cheeses to suit your taste.

Peel Me a Pizza

Using a pizza peel effectively takes a little practice. The peel must be well coated with flour or cornmeal to keep raw dough from sticking to the wood. A gentle back-and-forth motion of the paddle can tell you whether your pizza is sticking or not. Cooked pizza are more easily loaded onto the peel, but do keep a heavy-duty oven mitt over your free hand in case the pizza needs a little coaxing off the stone.

1. Roll or press pizza dough into 12-inch circle, slightly thicker at the edges than in the center. If using pizza pan, sprinkle the bottom with cornmeal or coat with olive oil and place dough in pan. If using a pizza stone, sprinkle with cornmeal and place stone in oven. Preheat oven to 400°F.
2. Spread ¾ cup sauce in the center of pizza, leaving edges bare.
3. In a large bowl, combine all the cheeses and toss gently to mix. Sprinkle half the cheese blend over the sauce on pizza, leaving edges bare.
4. If using a hot stone or tiles, use a well-floured pizza peel to carefully lift pizza from preparation surface and place on stone. Bake for 15 to 20 minutes or until the crust is lightly browned and cheese is melted.
5. Remove pizza from oven carefully (use peel if baking with a stone). Set aside to rest briefly before slicing.

Deep-Dish Cheese Pizza

Makes one 12-inch pizza

1 recipe Chicago Deep-Dish Crust dough (see recipe to follow)

3 cups shredded mozzarella cheese

1½ cups chunky tomato sauce

This recipe makes the most basic casserole-style pizza. Be sure to serve with forks and plenty of napkins.

1. Coat one 12-inch deep-dish pizza or pie pan with olive oil. Press dough into pan, making sure dough goes all the way up the sides of the pan. Preheat oven to 450°F.
2. Sprinkle mozzarella over the crust of pizza, using about half the mozzarella.
3. Pour 1 cup sauce in the center of pizza and spread evenly over the mozzarella. Sprinkle 1 cup of mozzarella evenly over the sauce. Spread remaining sauce over the cheese layer.
4. Sprinkle ½ cup mozzarella over the top of the pizza.
5. Reduce heat to 400°F and bake pizza for 20 to 25 minutes or until crust is light brown and centers are browned and bubbly.

CHICAGO DEEP-DISH CRUST

Makes crust for one 12-inch pizza

½ package active dry yeast

½ cup warm water, about 100°F

¼ tablespoon sugar

1¾ cup all-purpose flour

¼ cup cornmeal

½ teaspoon salt

⅛ cup, plus ½ tablespoons olive oil

1. Combine yeast, ½ cup water, sugar, and 1 cup flour in a large bowl. Stir, then cover and set aside for 15 to 20 minutes. Uncover and add remaining water, flour, cornmeal, salt, and ½ cup oil.

2. With a wooden spoon, stir ingredients until just blended. Turn mixture onto a well-floured nonstick surface and knead until shiny and elastic, about 10 minutes. Oil dough with olive oil, cover, and place in a warm spot to rise until doubled in size, about 2 hours.

3. Punch dough down and knead briefly. Divide into four equal portions. Press each portion into a well-oiled deep-dish pan. Let stand 10 to 20 minutes or until dough rises again. Press dough up sides of the pan and to a uniform thickness at the center. Fill and bake according to recipe instructions.

White Pizza

 Makes one 12-inch pizza

 Total Cost: $3.63

1 recipe California Thin Crust dough (see recipe to follow)

1 tablespoon cornmeal or 1 tablespoon oil

1 clove garlic, pressed

¼ cup extra virgin olive oil

⅛ teaspoon kosher salt

½ cup shredded mozzarella cheese

¼ cup shredded Parmesan cheese

¼ cup shredded Asiago cheese

This flavorful, simple pizza makes a great appetizer or cocktail snack when cut into thin slices. Be sure to use top quality oil and cheeses for best flavor.

1. Roll or press pizza dough into very thin 12-inch circle, slightly thicker at the edges than in the center. If using pizza pan, sprinkle the bottom with cornmeal or coat with oil and place dough in pan. If using a pizza stone, sprinkle with cornmeal and place rolled dough directly on stone.
2. Whisk pressed garlic into olive oil. Spread olive oil evenly over pizza. Sprinkle each with kosher salt.
3. In a large bowl, combine all the cheeses and toss gently to mix. Sprinkle half the cheese blend over the oil on pizza.
4. Place one pizza in the oven at 425°F. Bake 10 to 12 minutes or until crust is browned and cheese is melted. Repeat with remaining pizza.
5. Let pizza rest briefly, then slice with a sharp knife or pizza wheel.

CALIFORNIA THIN CRUST

Makes crust for one 12-inch pizza

$ Total Cost: $1.13

¼ packet active dry yeast

¼ cup warm water, about 100°F

½ tablespoon vegetable oil

½ teaspoon sugar

1½ cup high-protein flour

¼ teaspoon salt

1. In a large mixer bowl, combine water, yeast, oil, and sugar. Using a mixer with a dough hook, stir on low speed until the yeast dissolves and the mixture is well combined. Slowly add flour and salt. Continue stirring until a stiff ball of dough forms.
2. Place dough in a large (2-gallon) resealable plastic bag or place in a bowl and cover with plastic wrap. Refrigerate the dough for 24 hours. Remove from refrigerator and allow to come to cool room temperature.
3. Turn pizza onto a well-floured surface. Divide into four sections. (Return any sections that aren't being used to the refrigerator.) Roll sections into very thin circle, dusting liberally with flour as you go. Prick pizza crust several times with a fork and top according to recipe directions.

Ultra-Thin Pizza Crust
To get your pizza super-thin, use the California Thin Crust recipe and a pasta roller. Run strips of dough through the rollers and line them up, overlapping slightly on a well-oiled pizza pan. Smooth out the seams, prick the crust with a fork, then use as directed in your recipe.

Feta and Black Olive Pizza

 Makes one 12-inch pizza

 Total Cost: $4.42

1 recipe Classic Crust dough (Chapter 9)

1 tablespoon cornmeal or 1 tablespoon olive oil

½ cup tomato sauce

¾ cup shredded mozzarella cheese

1 cup crumbled feta cheese

½ cup chopped kalamata olives

⅛ cup fresh oregano leaves

Black pepper to taste

This pizza pays homage to Greece, the original home of meals prepared on an edible bread "plate."

1. Roll or press pizza dough into 12-inch circle, slightly thicker at the edges than in the center. If using pizza pan, sprinkle the bottom with cornmeal or coat with olive oil and place dough in pan. If using a pizza stone, sprinkle with cornmeal and place stone in oven. Preheat oven to 400°F.
2. Spread ¾ cup sauce in the center of pizza, leaving one inch around the edges bare.
3. Sprinkle ¾ cup mozzarella cheese over the sauce on pizza. Distribute 1 cup crumbled feta evenly over pizza, leaving edges bare. Evenly distribute olives and oregano leaves, then grind black pepper to taste over pizza.
4. If using a hot stone or tiles, use a well-floured pizza peel to carefully lift one pizza from preparation surface and place on stone. Bake for 15 to 20 minutes or until the crust is lightly browned and cheese is melted.
5. Remove pizza from oven carefully (use peel if baking with a stone). Set aside to rest briefly before slicing.

More on Mozzarella

Adding mozzarella to specialty cheese pizza like feta and Gorgonzola gives the pie more cheesy taste and texture without making the flavor overwhelming. If you're a hard-core pungent cheese fan, by all means up the proportion of your favorite variety.

Spicy Queso Pizza

Makes one 12-inch pizza

1 recipe Classic Crust dough (Chapter 9)

1 tablespoon cornmeal or 1 tablespoon olive oil

¼ cup tomato sauce

1 (5-ounce) can tomatoes with green chilis, drained

1½ cup crumbled processed cheese

½ cup shredded mozzarella cheese

This may not be the pizza you make for your ultrasophisticated friends, but it has comfort-food familiarity for those of us who grew up eating Ro-Tel dip.

1. Roll or press pizza dough into 12-inch circle, slightly thicker at the edges than in the center. If using pizza pan, sprinkle the bottom with cornmeal or coat with olive oil and place dough in pan. If using a pizza stone, sprinkle with cornmeal and place stone in oven. Preheat oven to 400°F.
2. Combine sauce and drained tomatoes with green chilis. Divide sauce over the pizza and spread from the center, leaving one inch around the edges bare.
3. Distribute 1½ cups crumbled processed cheese evenly over pizza, leaving edges bare. Sprinkle pizza with mozzarella.
4. If using a hot stone or tiles, use a well-floured pizza peel to carefully lift pizza from preparation surface and place on stone. Bake for 15 to 20 minutes or until the crust is lightly browned and cheese is melted.
5. Remove pizza from oven carefully (use peel if baking with a stone). Set aside to rest briefly before slicing.

Southern Pimiento Cheese Pizza

Makes one 12-inch pizza

1 recipe California Thin Crust dough (Chapter 9)

1½ tablespoon extra virgin olive oil

1 tablespoon cornmeal

1 cup prepared pimiento cheese

1 cup shredded mozzarella cheese

½ cup shredded Colby cheese

Every Southern cook knows of at least one family pimiento cheese recipe. You can buy this kitschy regional favorite in jars, but it just isn't the same as homemade.

1. Roll or press pizza dough into very thin 12-inch circle, slightly thicker at the edges than in the center. Divide 1 tablespoon olive oil over the bottom of pizza pan or large quiche pan. Sprinkle cornmeal over the oil.
2. Brush remaining olive oil evenly over pizza.
3. Preheat oven to 400°F. Place pizza pan in the oven and bake until crust is lightly browned, about 7 minutes. Remove pizza crust and let rest for 5 minutes.
4. Spread 1 cup of pimiento cheese over the top of pizza crust, followed by 1 cup of shredded mozzarella and ½ cup of shredded Colby.
5. Return pizza to the oven and bake just until shredded cheese has melted. Let pizza rest briefly, then slice with a sharp knife or pizza wheel.

Favorite Pimiento Cheese
In a food processor, combine 3 cups shredded Cheddar cheese, 4 ounces softened cream cheese, 1 cup mayonnaise, one 4-ounce jar drained diced pimiento, 1 tablespoon sugar, 1 teaspoon Worcestershire sauce, and a pinch of red pepper. Process until smooth and a uniform coral-pink color. Keep covered in the refrigerator until ready to use.

Herbed Cottage Cheese Pizza

Makes one 12-inch pizza

1 recipe Classic Crust dough (Chapter 9)

1 tablespoon cornmeal or 1 tablespoon olive oil

1 tablespoon extra virgin olive oil

1 clove garlic

½ green onion, chopped

⅛ cup parsley leaves

1 tablespoon fresh basil leaves

1 cup large-curd cottage cheese, drained

¼ teaspoon coarsely ground black pepper

1 cup shredded mozzarella cheese

The cottage cheese in this recipe retains its chunky texture. If you prefer a smoother topping, place drained cottage cheese in a food processor and pulse until it resembles ricotta.

1. Roll or press pizza dough into 12-inch circle, slightly thicker at the edges than in the center. If using pizza pan, sprinkle the bottom with cornmeal or coat with olive oil and place dough in pan. If using a pizza stone, sprinkle with cornmeal and place stone in oven. Preheat oven to 400°F.
2. Brush 1 tablespoon extra virgin olive oil over pizza, leaving edges bare. In a food processor or chopper, combine garlic, green onion, parsley, and basil. Pulse until minced.
3. Combine drained cottage cheese with herbs. Spread 1 cup cottage cheese over pizza, leaving one inch around the edges bare. Sprinkle coarsely ground pepper over the cottage cheese. Sprinkle 1 cup mozzarella over pizza.
4. If using a hot stone or tiles, use a well-floured pizza peel to carefully lift one pizza from preparation surface and place on stone. Bake for 15 to 20 minutes or until the crust is lightly browned and cheese is melted.
5. Remove pizza from oven carefully (use peel if baking with a stone). Set aside to rest briefly before slicing.

Rustic Repasts

Instead of same-old chicken salad sandwiches, treat guests at your next luncheon event to a warm, crusty cheese pizza and a salad of greens tossed with balsamic vinaigrette. If you don't have time to make from-scratch crust, just start with a good ready-made variety. For dessert, try berries and a dollop of crème fraiche or whipped cream.

Chopped Salad Pizza

Makes one 12-inch pizza

1 recipe California Thin Crust dough (Chapter 9)

1½ tablespoon olive oil

1 tablespoon cornmeal

1 cup tomato sauce

¼ cup finely diced carrots

¼ cup finely diced celery

¼ cup finely diced red onion

⅓ cup finely diced zucchini

⅓ cup finely chopped mushrooms

¼ cup minced fresh herbs

2 cups mozzarella crumbles

Choose any herbs you like to give this pizza a signature flavor. A mix of parsley, green onion, and basil is a great place to start.

1. Roll or press pizza dough into thin 12-inch circle, slightly thicker at the edges than in the center. Divide 1 tablespoon olive oil over the bottom of pizza pan or large quiche pan. Sprinkle cornmeal over the oil.
2. Preheat oven to 400°F. Place pizza pan in the oven and bake until crust is lightly browned, about 7 minutes. Remove from the oven and spoon 1 cup of tomato sauce over pizza.
3. Combine carrots, celery, onion, zucchini, and mushrooms in a bowl. Toss with remaining olive oil until vegetables are coated. Divide vegetables evenly over pizza.
4. Sprinkle fresh herbs evenly over the top of the vegetables. Top pizza with 2 cups of mozzarella cheese.
5. Return pizza to the oven and bake until shredded cheese has melted and crust darken slightly, about 5 to 7 minutes. Let pizza rest briefly, then slice with a sharp knife or pizza wheel.

Lunch Crunch

Warmed but still crisp salad veggies give pizza a unique texture that's perfect for lunch or a hearty mid-afternoon tea offering. Serve with a cup of creamy squash or tomato bisque for a vegetarian feast.

Wild Mushroom Melt Pizza

Makes one 12-inch pizza

$ Total Cost: $4.48

1 recipe Classic Crust dough (Chapter 9)

1 tablespoon cornmeal or 1 tablespoon olive oil

¾ cup tomato sauce

1 tablespoon unsalted butter

1 clove garlic, minced

2 cups mixed wild mushrooms, coarsely chopped

⅛ cup minced fresh parsley

1½ cups shredded mozzarella cheese

A mix of different types of mushrooms give this pizza layers of flavor and texture. For an artistic pie, distribute mushroom slices, flat mushrooms, and chopped mushrooms in an alternating pattern.

1. Roll or press pizza dough into 12-inch circle, slightly thicker at the edges than in the center. If using pizza pan, sprinkle the bottom with cornmeal or coat with olive oil and place dough in pan. If using a pizza stone, sprinkle with cornmeal and place stone in oven. Preheat oven to 400°F.
2. Spread ¾ cup sauce in the center of pizza, leaving one inch around the edges bare.
3. In a large skillet, heat 2 tablespoons butter until bubbling. Add garlic and mushrooms and sauté until mushrooms are crisp-tender. Sprinkle with parsley.
4. With a slotted spoon, remove mushrooms from the skillet, draining as much liquid as possible. Distribute mushrooms evenly over pizza sauce.
5. Sprinkle ½ cup mozzarella cheese over the mushrooms. Then spread remaining cup mozzarella evenly over pizza, leaving edges bare.
6. If using a hot stone or tiles, use a well-floured pizza peel to carefully lift one pizza from preparation surface and place on stone. Bake for 15 to 20 minutes or until the crust is lightly browned and cheese is melted.
7. Remove pizza from oven carefully (use peel if baking with a stone). Set aside to rest briefly before slicing.

Heirloom Tomato Pizza

 Makes one 12-inch pizza

1 recipe Focaccia Crust dough (Chapter 9)

1 tablespoon olive oil

½ cup tomato sauce

1½ cup shredded mozzarella cheese

3½ medium heirloom tomatoes, thinly sliced

¼ cup fresh basil ribbons

Freshly ground black pepper to taste

This pizza combines the classic flavors of creamy fresh mozzarella, sweet tomatoes, and basil with a substantial breadlike crust.

1. Roll focaccia dough into a 12-inch circle. Grease deep-dish pizza pan with olive oil and press dough into the pan. Bake at 400°F for 15 minutes, or until focaccias have just begun to brown.
2. Remove from oven and carefully spread tomato sauce over crust. Sprinkle with Parmesan cheese. Distribute 1 cup of the mozzarella evenly over the pizza. Arrange tomato slices in overlapping concentric circles over the cheese, then sprinkle remaining diced mozzarella over tomatoes.
3. Sprinkle basil ribbons over pizza and add freshly ground black pepper to taste.
4. Return pan to oven and bake for 10 minutes, or just long enough for mozzarella to melt and tomato slices to become warm and soft.
5. Remove from oven and let stand for a few minutes before slicing.

Vintage Beauties

Heirloom tomatoes come in a beautiful array of colors, ranging from pale green to orange to crimson, with plenty of mottled or striped varieties in between. Pick vine-ripened tomatoes in different shades for an eye-catching dish. Warmed heirloom tomatoes taste like summer on a plate.

The $5 Takeout Cookbook

Spinach-Artichoke Pie

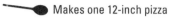

Makes one 12-inch pizza

1 recipe Pan Pizza Crust dough
(see recipe to follow)

1 tablespoon olive oil

¾ cup tomato sauce

½ pound spinach leaves,
stemmed and washed

½ teaspoon minced garlic

½ tablespoon butter

¾ cup coarsely chopped
cooked artichoke bottoms

1½ cup mozzarella cheese

Freshly ground black pepper

If you have the time and energy to boil and clean fresh artichokes, by all means do so. Otherwise, frozen or canned artichoke bottoms will work just fine for this pizza.

1. Roll pizza dough into a circle large enough to cover bottom and sides of 12-inch pizza or quiche pan. Spread a tablespoon of olive oil over the bottom of pan, then press dough circle into the pan.
2. Ladle ¾ cup of sauce into pan and spread evenly over the crust.
3. In a large, flat-bottomed wok or Dutch oven, combine washed spinach leaves, garlic, and butter. Sauté just until spinach has wilted. Remove spinach to a fine sieve and press out as much liquid as possible.
4. Distribute cooked spinach evenly over pizza crust, then sprinkle artichokes evenly over the spinach.
5. Spread mozzarella over pizza. Add freshly ground black pepper to taste. Bake pan in a preheated oven at 400°F until crust has browned and cheese is bubbly, about 20 minutes.

PAN PIZZA CRUST

 Makes crust for one 12-inch pizza

Total Cost: $0.84

½ cup reduced-fat milk | 1 tablespoon sugar
½ package active dry yeast | ¼ teaspoon salt
1½ cup all-purpose flour | 1¼ tablespoon olive oil

Pan pizza crust is extremely rich. To achieve the flaky exterior crust many pizza-lovers prize, use a generous amount of olive oil to coat the pan when making your pan pizza.

1. Warm milk in the microwave to about 100°F, or just warm, not hot, to the touch.
2. In the bowl of a mixer with a dough hook, combine yeast, flour, sugar, and salt. Stir to combine. With dough hook running on low speed, slowly add the warm milk followed by 4 tablespoons olive oil.
3. Turn mixer to medium-low or proper speed for kneading. Allow mixer to knead the dough for 5 minutes or until mixture is slightly glossy and springy to the touch. If the dough seems too wet, add a small amount of flour and knead a little longer.
4. Remove dough to a lightly floured work surface. A pastry board or silicone baking sheet is good. Waxed paper or nonstick foil on the counter will do. Shape dough into a ball. Grease a metal or glass bowl with the remaining olive oil and place the dough ball in the bowl, turning to lightly oil the dough.
5. Cover the bowl with plastic wrap and place in a warm spot. Allow dough to rise 30 minutes or until doubled in size. Punch down. Lightly pat into a flattened circle, cover, and let stand 20 to 30 minutes before placing in pan. Refrigerated dough should be allowed to come to room temperature before using.

Roasted Peppers and Caramelized Onion Pie

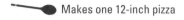 Makes one 12-inch pizza

$ Total Cost: $4.71

1 large Vidalia onion, sliced

1½ tablespoon butter

¼ teaspoon sugar

½ large green bell pepper

½ large red bell pepper

1 recipe California Thin Crust dough (Chapter 9)

1 tablespoon olive oil or 2 tablespoons cornmeal

½ cup tomato sauce

½ cup Asiago cheese (optional)

Freshly ground black pepper to taste

This pie pays homage to the French *pissaladière*, a crust topped with olive oil, onions, and anchovies. It can easily go cheeseless for those who want a dairy-free dish.

1. In a large skillet or Dutch oven, combine onions, butter, and sugar. Cook over medium heat, stirring often, until onions turn a rich brown.
2. To roast peppers, hold over a hot grill or open flame with a long-handled fork until skin is charred and blistered. (If it's more convenient, peppers can be cored and halved, then roasted on a rack in the oven until skin chars.) Place peppers in a paper or resealable plastic bag and close loosely. Allow to cool for 10 to 15 minutes, then peel off the charred skin. Core and seed peppers and cut into vertical strips.
3. Roll dough into two 12-inch circles, slightly thicker at the edges than in the center. If using pizza pan, sprinkle the bottom with cornmeal or coat with olive oil and place dough in pan. If using a pizza stone, sprinkle with cornmeal and place stone in oven. Preheat oven to 400°F.
4. Spread a thin layer of pizza sauce over each crust, leaving one inch around the edges bare. Sprinkle pizza with Asiago cheese, if desired. Spread a tangle of caramelized onions over the sauce. Arrange strips of roasted peppers in alternating colors in a spoke pattern over the pizza.
5. Bake pizza, one at a time if necessary, at 400°F in the center of the oven for 15 minutes or until browned. Remove and let stand for 5 minutes, then slice and serve.

Sun-Dried Tomato and Ricotta Pizza

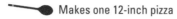 Makes one 12-inch pizza

1 recipe Honey-Wheat Crust dough (see recipe to follow)

1 tablespoon cornmeal or 1 tablespoon olive oil

1 tablespoon extra virgin olive oil

1 clove garlic, minced

1 cup whole-milk ricotta cheese

⅔ cup finely chopped sun-dried tomatoes

1 tablespoon fresh basil ribbons

Black pepper to taste

1 cup shredded mozzarella cheese

For this recipe, use oil-packed dried tomatoes. Buy a commercial brand or make your own by marinating dry-packed tomatoes in olive oil and your favorite herbs. Cover and refrigerate for a few days before using.

1. Roll or press pizza dough into 12-inch circle, slightly thicker at the edges than in the center. If using pizza pan, sprinkle the bottom with cornmeal or coat with olive oil and place dough in pan. If using a pizza stone, sprinkle with cornmeal and place stone in oven. Preheat oven to 400°F.
2. Brush 1 tablespoon extra virgin olive oil over pizza, leaving edges bare. Sprinkle minced garlic evenly over the oil.
3. Combine ricotta with sun-dried tomatoes, basil, and black pepper. Spread half the ricotta mixture over pizza, leaving edges bare. Sprinkle 1½ cups mozzarella over pizza.
4. If using a hot stone or tiles, use a well-floured pizza peel to carefully lift one pizza from preparation surface and place on stone. Bake for 15 to 20 minutes or until the crust is lightly browned and cheese is melted.
5. Remove pizza from oven carefully (use peel if baking with a stone). Set aside to rest briefly before slicing.

HONEY-WHEAT CRUST

 Makes crust for one 12-inch pizza

Total Cost: $0.76

½ package active dry yeast

½ cup warm water, about 110°F

½ tablespoon honey

¼ teaspoon sugar

½ teaspoon salt

¾ cup bread flour

¾ cup whole-wheat flour

½ tablespoon olive oil

Use this crust for a hint of hearty whole-wheat flavor. It's a great option for those transitioning to healthy carbs and pizza lovers who want variety without a too-heavy dose of coarse grains.

1. In a large measuring cup, dissolve yeast in water. Let stand 5 minutes or until bubbly. Add honey to liquid. Combine sugar, salt, and both flours in the bowl of a mixer with a dough hook. Or, to mix by hand, place in a large bowl. Make a well in the flour mixture and pour in the water, followed by 1 tablespoon of oil.

2. Turn the mixer on low to blend, or begin stirring the flour into the liquid with a wooden spoon, a little at a time. When ingredients are well combined, turn the mixer on medium-low to knead for 5 minutes. If working dough by hand, turn the dough onto a well-floured work surface. Use a pressing motion with the heels of your hands to push and stretch the dough. Work dough until mixture is slightly shiny and not too sticky to the touch.

3. The kneaded dough should be divided into four equal pieces. Store any dough not being used in a resealable bag in the refrigerator. Oil remaining dough and place in a bowl, covered, to rise for 1 hour. Punch the dough down, shape into a disk, and let rest for 30 minutes.

4. Grab dough by the edges, turning the disk a few inches at a time, allowing gravity to stretch the dough without tearing. Roll the dough into a crust shape or press into a pizza pan. Top as directed in recipe.

Eggplant Parmesan Pizza

 Makes one 12-inch pizza

¼ medium eggplant, sliced horizontally ¼-inch thick

½ to 1 teaspoons coarse salt

1 egg

⅛ cup milk

½ cup fine seasoned bread crumbs

⅛ cup grated Parmesan cheese

Vegetable oil for frying

1 recipe Classic Crust dough (Chapter 9)

1 tablespoon olive oil

½ cup chunky tomato sauce

1¼ cups shredded mozzarella cheese

To make this pie with fewer calories, don't batter and fry the eggplant slices. Instead, spritz slices with cooking spray and bake at 400°F until slightly softened. Then use as directed on pizza.

1. Discard ends of eggplant. Sprinkle slices with coarse salt and set in a sieve or on paper towels to drain for 20 minutes. Rinse salt from eggplant slices and pat dry with paper towels.
2. Whisk together eggs and milk. Mix together bread crumbs and grated parmesan in a large bowl or pie pan. Dip each eggplant slice in egg mixture and coat lightly with seasoned bread crumb mixture.
3. In a large skillet, pour oil to a depth of about 2 inches. Heat over medium-high heat until a drop of water sizzles in the oil. Fry eggplant slices, a few at a time, until browned. Drain on paper towels.
4. Roll out a circle of pie crust dough. Spread olive oil in a 12-inch deep-dish pizza or pie pan. Press dough circle into pan and prick bottom a few times with a fork. Ladle tomato sauce into pan, followed by 1 cup of mozzarella cheese.
5. Arrange fried eggplant slices over the cheese, overlapping as necessary. Sprinkle remaining mozzarella over the eggplant slices. Bake at 400°F until browned and bubbly, about 20 minutes.

Veggie-Sausage, Peppers, and Mushrooms Pizza

 Makes one 12-inch pizza

½ tablespoon butter

½ clove garlic, minced

2 vegetable-based sausage patties, chopped

¼ pound sliced white mushrooms

½ green bell pepper, cored and diced

⅛ cup minced parsley

1 recipe Classic Crust dough (Chapter 9)

1 tablespoon cornmeal or 1 tablespoon olive oil

¾ cup tomato sauce

1½ cup shredded mozzarella cheese

1. In a large skillet over medium-high heat, melt butter. Add garlic and vegetable-based sausage and cook until sausage pieces become browned. Combine sausage with mushrooms, peppers, and parsley.
2. Roll or press pizza dough into 12-inch circle, slightly thicker at the edges than in the center. If using pizza pan, sprinkle the bottom with cornmeal or coat with olive oil and place dough in pan. If using a pizza stone, sprinkle with cornmeal and place stone in oven. Preheat oven to 400°F.
3. Spread ¾ cup sauce in the center of pizza, leaving edges bare.
4. Distribute 1½ cups mozzarella evenly over pizza, leaving edges bare. Spread sausage mixture evenly over cheese on pizza.
5. If using a hot stone or tiles, use a well-floured pizza peel to carefully lift pizza from preparation surface and place on stone. If using pizza pan, place pizza in the center of the oven. Bake for 15 to 20 minutes or until the crust is lightly browned and cheese is melted.
6. Remove pizza from oven carefully (use peel if baking with a stone). Set aside to rest briefly before slicing.

Meatless Meat

Meat clones made from soy or other vegetable protein can be a godsend to carnivores trying to switch to a vegetarian diet or for gatherings that include meat and nonmeat eaters. However, some products taste more "real" than others. Sample a few products before serving them to family and friends.

Broccoli and Fontina Cheese Pizza

Makes one 12-inch pizza

1 recipe Classic Crust dough (Chapter 9)

1 tablespoon cornmeal or 1 tablespoon olive oil

¾ cup tomato sauce

½ cup shredded mozzarella cheese

2 cups small broccoli florets, blanched

½ cup finely diced fontina cheese

Freshly ground black pepper to taste

For nonvegetarian meals, add crumbled bacon or finely diced ham to this pizza for a salty, smoky accent.

1. Roll or press pizza dough into 12-inch circle, slightly thicker at the edges than in the center. If using pizza pan, sprinkle the bottom with cornmeal or coat with olive oil and place dough in pan. If using a pizza stone, sprinkle with cornmeal and place stone in oven. Preheat oven to 400°F.
2. Spread ¾ cup sauce in the center of pizza, leaving one inch around the edges bare.
3. Sprinkle 1 cup mozzarella cheese over the sauce on pizza. Distribute 2 cups broccoli florets evenly over pizza, leaving edges bare. Top with 1 cup diced fontina sprinkled over pizza. Add pepper to taste.
4. If using a hot stone or tiles, use a well-floured pizza peel to carefully lift one pizza from preparation surface and place on stone. Bake for 15 to 20 minutes or until the crust is lightly browned and cheese is melted.
5. Remove pizza from oven carefully (use peel if baking with a stone). Set aside to rest briefly before slicing.

Roasted Cauliflower Pizza

 Makes one 12-inch pizza

2 cups cauliflower florets

1½ tablespoon extra virgin olive oil

1 clove garlic, pressed

½ teaspoon white balsamic vinegar

Salt and pepper to taste

1 tablespoon olive oil

1 recipe California Thin Crust dough (Chapter 9)

¾ cup tomato sauce

1 cup shredded mozzarella cheese

Roasted cauliflower can be made ahead of time and stored in the refrigerator for a few hours or overnight until you're ready to make the pizza.

1. Preheat oven to 425°F. Toss cauliflower florets with oil, garlic, vinegar, salt, and pepper. Roast for 12 to 15 minutes, stirring occasionally. Remove from oven. When cool, break into smaller florets.
2. Coat two 12-inch pizza pan with olive oil. Roll out or press dough into pan to cover the bottoms. Spread ¾ cup sauce over pizza, then distribute roasted cauliflower over pizza.
3. Sprinkle mozzarella over cauliflower. Bake pizza in a 400°F oven for 15 minutes or until crust is browned. Let stand 5 minutes, then slice with a sharp knife or pizza cutter.

Chopped Herb and Roasted Plum Tomato Pizza

 Makes one 12-inch pizza

$ Total Cost: $4.80

8 plum tomatoes, halved vertically

⅛ cup plus 2 tablespoons olive oil

1 clove garlic

1 green onions, trimmed

¼ cup fresh parsley leaves

⅛ cup fresh basil leaves

1 tablespoon fresh oregano leaves

½ tablespoon fresh sage leaves

1 teaspoon fresh thyme leaves

Salt and pepper to taste

1 recipe Classic Crust dough (Chapter 9)

2 cups mozzarella cheese

1. Coat halved tomatoes with ¼ cup olive oil. Place on a sheet of nonstick foil on a baking pan and roast tomatoes at 400°F for 25 minutes. Set aside and allow tomatoes to cool slightly.
2. Place garlic, green onions, parsley, basil, oregano, sage, and thyme in a food processor. Pulse until herbs are all finely chopped. Spoon into a large bowl. Place roasted tomatoes in food processor and pulse until coarsely chopped. Add to bowl with herbs and toss until well blended. Add salt and pepper to taste.
3. Coat 12-inch deep-dish pizza or pie pan with remaining olive oil. Divide dough and press into pan, making sure dough goes all the way up the sides of the pan.
4. Sprinkle mozzarella over the crust of pizza. Spoon tomato-herb mixture into each crust, spreading to cover the cheese.
5. Sprinkle remaining mozzarella evenly over the pies. Bake pizza for 20 to 25 minutes or until crust is light brown and centers are browned and bubbly. Let stand for 5 minutes before cutting into wedges.

Plum Perfect

Plum tomatoes are meatier than other tomato varieties. When roasted, plums give off less liquid and yield more usable, sweet-tasting pulp. Grape tomatoes, which are essentially miniature plums, can be roasted as well.

The $5 Takeout Cookbook

CHAPTER 10

CHICKEN

Shredded Barbecued Chicken Pizza

 Makes one 12-inch pizza

1 recipe Classic Crust dough (Chapter 9)

1 tablespoon cornmeal or 1 tablespoon olive oil

1 cup barbecue sauce

¾ cup shredded Cheddar or Colby cheese

¾ cup shredded Monterey jack cheese

1½ cup shredded roasted or poached chicken

¼ cup sliced green onion

This is a great way to give leftover chicken a makeover. You can also substitute duck or turkey for the chicken, or do a quick fix by purchasing already-roasted chicken at the supermarket.

1. Roll or press pizza dough into 12-inch circle, slightly thicker at the edges than in the center. If using pizza pan, sprinkle the bottom with cornmeal or coat with olive oil and place dough in pan. If using a pizza stone, sprinkle with cornmeal and place stone in oven. Preheat oven to 400°F.
2. Spread ¾ cup barbecue sauce in the center of pizza, leaving edges bare.
3. Sprinkle 1 cup Cheddar or Colby over the sauce on pizza. Distribute ¾ cup Monterey jack evenly over pizza, leaving edges bare.
4. Toss remaining ¼ cup barbecue sauce with shredded chicken. Spread chicken evenly over the cheese on pizza. Sprinkle sliced green onions over pizza.
5. If using a hot stone or tiles, use a well-floured pizza peel to carefully lift pizza from preparation surface and place on stone. If using pizza pan, place pizza in the center of the oven. Bake for 15 to 20 minutes or until the crust is lightly browned and toppings are bubbly.
6. Remove pizza from oven carefully (use peel if baking with a stone). Set aside to rest briefly before slicing.

Hawaiian Pizza

Makes one 12-inch pizza

1 recipe Classic Crust dough (Chapter 9)

1 tablespoon cornmeal or 1 tablespoon olive oil

1 cup tomato sauce

½ tablespoon brown sugar

½ tablespoon soy sauce

1¾ cup shredded mozzarella cheese

1 cup diced grilled or pan-seared chicken breast

½ cup diced green bell pepper

½ cup diced fresh or canned pineapple

¼ cup diced red onion

⅛ cup minced parsley

Chicken breast that's been grilled over hot coals gives the pizza a wonderful smoky-sweet flavor. Next time you cook out, make extra for pizza the next day.

1. Roll or press pizza dough into 12-inch circle, slightly thicker at the edges than in the center. If using pizza pan, sprinkle the bottom with cornmeal or coat with olive oil and place dough in pan. If using a pizza stone, sprinkle with cornmeal and place stone in oven. Preheat oven to 400°F.
2. In a bowl, combine tomato sauce, brown sugar, and soy sauce. Whisk to blend. Spread half the sauce in the center of pizza, leaving edges bare.
3. Sprinkle mozzarella evenly over pizza, leaving one inch around the edges bare.
4. Dot pizza with 1 cup diced chicken breast, followed by ½ cup bell pepper and ½ cup pineapple. Sprinkle onion and parsley over pizza.
5. If baking on a hot stone or tiles, use a well-floured pizza peel to carefully lift pizza from preparation surface and place on stone. If using pizza pan, place first in the center of the oven. Bake for 15 to 20 minutes or until the crust is lightly browned and toppings are bubbly.
6. Remove pizza from oven carefully (use peel if baking with a stone). Set aside to rest briefly before slicing.

Chicken and Broccoli Pizza

Makes one 12-inch pizza

1 recipe Classic Crust dough (Chapter 9)

1 tablespoon olive oil

1 tablespoon cornmeal

¾ cup soy sauce

1 cup shredded mozzarella cheese

1 pan-seared boneless chicken breast half, sliced crosswise

1 cup small broccoli florets, blanched

⅛ cup minced green onion

1 teaspoon sesame seeds

1. Roll or press pizza dough into thin 12-inch circle, slightly thicker at the edges than in the center. Divide 1 tablespoon olive oil over the bottom of pizza pan or large quiche pan. Sprinkle cornmeal over the oil.
2. Preheat oven to 400°F. Spread 1 cup soy sauce over each crust, leaving edges bare. Divide mozzarella evenly over pizza.
3. Toss chicken breast slices in soy sauce and divide chicken over pizza, followed by broccoli florets and green onion.
4. Sprinkle pizza with sesame seeds.
5. Place pizza in the oven and bake until cheese has melted and crust are browned, about 10 to 12 minutes. Let pizza rest briefly, then slice with a sharp knife or pizza wheel.

Chicken Alfredo Pizza

 Makes one 12-inch pizza

$ Total Cost: $4.94

1 recipe Pan Pizza Crust dough (Chapter 9)

1 tablespoon olive oil

¾ cup Alfredo sauce

1 chicken breast half, poached and diced

½ teaspoon minced garlic

½ tablespoon butter

½ cup coarsely chopped white mushrooms

1¼ cup mozzarella cheese

Freshly ground black pepper

Mushrooms give this pizza added substance. If you'd rather not have them, feel free to add another vegetable or more chicken to the pizza.

1. Roll pizza dough into two circles large enough to cover bottom and sides of 12-inch pizza or quiche pan. Spread a tablespoon of olive oil over the bottom of each pan, then press dough circle into the pan.
2. Ladle ¾ cup of sauce into each pan and spread evenly over the crust. Divide diced chicken and distribute over pizza.
3. In a large, flat-bottomed wok or Dutch oven, combine garlic, butter, and mushrooms. Sauté 3 to 5 minutes or until mushrooms soften. Remove mushrooms with a slotted spoon and spread over chicken.
4. Spread cheese over pizza. Add freshly ground black pepper to taste. Bake pan in a preheated oven at 400°F until crust has browned and cheese is bubbly, about 20 minutes.

Whither Alfredo?

Around 1914, Roman restaurateur Alfredo di Lelio created a dish of supremely thin, tender egg noodles, extra-rich butter, and freshly grated Parmesan cheese. He served it with a flourish, brandishing golden cutlery, and named it Fettuccine all'Alfredo. Eventually, the rest of the world began calling any white Parmesan sauce-laced dish "Alfredo." However, in Rome, the name still refers to a specific dish.

Chicken Fajita Pizza

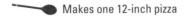 Makes one 12-inch pizza

1 recipe Classic Crust dough (Chapter 9)

1 tablespoon cornmeal or 1 tablespoon olive oil

¼ cup Refried Bean Spread (see recipe to follow)

⅓ cup picante sauce

½ cup shredded Cheddar or Colby cheese

½ cup shredded Monterey jack cheese

1 grilled chicken breast, sliced into thin strips

½ small green bell pepper, cored and cut into strips

½ small red bell pepper, cored and cut into strips

½ sweet onion, trimmed and cut into strips

¼ cup diced tomatoes

⅛ cup minced cilantro

If you have time, place halved peppers and onion on the grill for a few minutes to get the slightly charred, smoky flavor of fajita veggies.

1. Roll or press pizza dough into 12-inch circle, slightly thicker at the edges than in the center. If using pizza pan, sprinkle the bottom with cornmeal or coat with olive oil and place dough in pan. If using a pizza stone, sprinkle with cornmeal and place stone in oven. Preheat oven to 400°F.
2. Spread ¼ cup Refried Bean Spread in the center of pizza, leaving edges bare. Top bean spread with Picante Sauce.
3. Sprinkle ½ cup Cheddar or Colby over the sauce on pizza. Distribute ½ cup Monterey jack evenly over pizza, leaving one inch around the edges bare.
4. Spread chicken evenly over the cheese on pizza. Sprinkle peppers, onions, and diced tomatoes over the pizza, followed by cilantro.
5. If baking on a hot stone or tiles, use a well-floured pizza peel to carefully lift pizza from preparation surface and place on stone. If using pizza pan, place pizza in the center of the oven. Bake for 15 to 20 minutes or until the crust is lightly browned and toppings are bubbly.
6. Remove pizza from oven carefully (use peel if baking with a stone). Set aside to rest briefly before slicing.

REFRIED BEAN SPREAD

 Makes 1 cup

$ Total Cost: $0.74

½ (15-ounce) cans refried
beans

⅛ cup chunky commercial
salsa

Pinch cumin

1. In a saucepan or microwave-safe bowl, warm the refried
   beans until softened and easy to stir.
2. Stir in salsa and cumin, mixing until well blended. Spread
   beans over pizza crust as directed in recipes.

Southwest Chicken Pizza

 Makes one 12-inch pizza

1 recipe Classic Crust dough (Chapter 9)

1 tablespoon cornmeal or 1 tablespoon olive oil

¾ cup picante sauce

½ cup shredded Cheddar or Colby cheese

½ cup shredded Monterey jack cheese

1 cup diced mesquite-grilled or smoked chicken breast

¼ cup black beans, drained

¼ cup roasted corn

¼ cup diced red or green bell pepper

¼ cup finely chopped red onion

¼ cup minced cilantro

Serve this whole-meal pizza with a dollop of sour cream and extra picante sauce on the side. Use ready-to-eat mesquite-flavored or smoked chicken from the supermarket to save time.

1. Roll or press pizza dough into 12-inch circle, slightly thicker at the edges than in the center. If using pizza pan, sprinkle the bottom with cornmeal or coat with olive oil and place dough in pan. If using a pizza stone, sprinkle with cornmeal and place stone in oven. Preheat oven to 400°F.
2. Spread ¾ cup picante sauce in the center of pizza, leaving edges bare.
3. Sprinkle ½ cup Cheddar or Colby over the sauce on pizza. Distribute 1 cup Monterey jack evenly over pizza, leaving one inch around the edges bare.
4. Spread chicken evenly over the cheese on pizza. Sprinkle black beans, corn, bell pepper, onion, and cilantro over the chicken.
5. If baking on a hot stone or tiles, use a well-floured pizza peel to carefully lift pizza from preparation surface and place on stone. If using pizza pan, place pizza in the center of the oven. Bake for 15 to 20 minutes or until the crust is lightly browned and toppings are bubbly.
6. Remove pizza from oven carefully (use peel if baking with a stone). Set aside to rest briefly before slicing.

Chicken and Artichoke Pizza

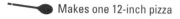 Makes one 12-inch pizza

1 recipe Classic Crust dough (Chapter 9)

1 tablespoon cornmeal or ½ tablespoon olive oil

¾ cup tomato sauce

1¼ cup shredded mozzarella cheese

6 ounces cooked artichoke hearts, quartered

1 cup cooked, diced chicken

Freshly ground black pepper to taste

1. Roll or press pizza dough into 12-inch circle, slightly thicker at the edges than in the center. If using pizza pan, sprinkle the bottom with cornmeal or coat with olive oil and place dough in pan. If using a pizza stone, sprinkle with cornmeal and place stone in oven. Preheat oven to 400°F.
2. Spread ¾ cup sauce in the center of pizza, leaving one inch around the edges bare.
3. Sprinkle ½ cup of mozzarella over the sauce on pizza. Distribute artichoke heart quarters evenly over pizza, leaving edges bare. Top with diced chicken. Sprinkle remaining mozzarella. Add pepper to taste.
4. If baking with a hot stone or tiles, use a well-floured pizza peel to carefully lift one pizza from preparation surface and place on stone. Bake for 15 to 20 minutes or until the crust is lightly browned and cheese is melted.
5. Remove pizza from oven carefully (use peel if baking with a stone). Set aside to rest briefly before slicing.

Grilled Chicken Pesto Pizza

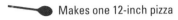 Makes one 12-inch pizza

1 recipe Classic Crust dough
(Chapter 9)

1 tablespoon olive oil

1 tablespoon cornmeal

½ cup pesto sauce

1 ¼ cup shredded mozzarella
cheese

1 grilled boneless chicken
breast half, sliced crosswise

⅛ cup toasted pine nuts

⅛ cup fresh basil ribbons

This pizza features classic fresh basil pesto sauce. If you prefer a pesto made with other herbs, or even a sun-dried-tomato pesto, feel free to experiment.

1. Roll or press pizza dough into thin 12-inch circle, slightly thicker at the edges than in the center. Drizzle 1 tablespoon olive oil over the bottom of pizza pan or large quiche pan. Sprinkle cornmeal over the oil.
2. Preheat oven to 400°F. Place pizza pan in oven and prick in several places with a fork. Bake until crust is lightly browned, about 7 minutes. Remove from oven and spoon or brush ½ cup pesto sauce over pizza.
3. Divide mozzarella evenly over pizza, followed by chicken breast slices, pine nuts, and basil ribbons.
4. Sprinkle cheese evenly over the pizza.
5. Return pizza to the oven and bake until shredded cheese has melted and crust darken slightly, about 5 to 7 minutes. Let pizza rest briefly, then slice with a sharp knife or pizza wheel.

Chicken and Fresh Tomato Pizza

 Makes one 12-inch pizza

$ Total Cost: $4.94

1 recipe Focaccia Crust dough (see recipe to follow)

1 tablespoon olive oil

½ cup tomato sauce

1⅔ cup shredded fresh mozzarella cheese

1½ cup grape tomatoes, halved lengthwise

1 grilled chicken breast half, diced

⅛ cup fresh basil ribbons

Freshly ground black pepper to taste

This pizza captures some of the favorite flavors of summer—grilled chicken, fresh tomatoes, and fresh herbs—on a dense bread crust.

1. Roll focaccia dough into a 12-inch circle. Grease deep-dish pizza pan with olive oil and press dough into the pan. Bake at 400°F for 15 minutes, or until focaccia has just begun to brown.

2. Remove from oven and spread tomato sauce over each crust. Distribute 1 cup mozzarella evenly over the pizza. Dot pizza with grape tomato halves, followed by the diced chicken, basil ribbons, and the remainder of the mozzarella.

3. Add freshly ground black pepper to taste. Return pan to oven and bake for 10 minutes, or just long enough for mozzarella to melt and tomatoes to soften. Remove from oven and let stand for a few minutes before slicing.

FOCACCIA CRUST

Makes crust for one 12-inch pizza

½ package active dry yeast

¼ cup warm water, about 100°F

2 ¼ cups bread flour

¼ teaspoon sugar

½ teaspoon salt

⅛ cup olive oil

½ tablespoon extra virgin olive oil

¼ teaspoon dried Italian herb blend

For pizza, focaccia loaves should be split in half horizontally, with each round serving as a pizza crust. Whole loaves can be topped with oil, herbs, and hard cheese—but saucy toppings will slide off.

1. Dissolve the yeast in water and let stand for 5 minutes. In a large bowl, combine flour, sugar, and salt. Slowly add the yeast, water, and oil. Stir until ingredients are well blended. Sprinkle on dried herbs.
2. Turn focaccia dough onto a well-floured surface and knead with the heels of your hands for 10 minutes. Place dough on a dry surface and cover with a large bowl. Let stand in a warm place for at least 1 hour.
3. Punch the dough down. Smooth dough into well oiled pizza pan. Brush top with olive oil and let stand for 1 hour. Bake focaccia in a 400°F preheated oven for 15 to 20 minutes. Remove from oven and let cool.
4. To use as pizza crust, split focaccia and top as directed in recipe. Return to oven if necessary to heat toppings.

Cashew Chicken Pizza

 Makes one 12-inch pizza

1 recipe California Thin Crust dough (Chapter 9)

1 tablespoon cornmeal or 1 tablespoon oil

⅓ cup soy sauce

⅛ cup chopped fresh cilantro

1 chicken breast half, cooked and diced

½ cup roasted cashews

Freshly ground black pepper to taste

1½ cup shredded mozzarella cheese

Nuts give pizza texture and an earthy flavor. For variety, try substituting slivered almonds for the cashews.

1. Roll or press pizza dough into a very thin 12-inch circle, slightly thicker at the edges than in the center. If using pizza pan, sprinkle the bottom with cornmeal or coat with oil and place dough in pan. If using a pizza stone, sprinkle with cornmeal and place rolled dough directly on stone.
2. Spread ⅓ cup soy sauce evenly over pizza. Sprinkle cilantro over the sauce.
3. Distribute the chicken and cashews over the sauce on pizza. Sprinkle with freshly ground black pepper, followed by the mozzarella cheese.
4. Place one pizza in the oven at 425°F. Bake 10 to 12 minutes or until crust is browned and cheese is melted.
5. Let pizza rest briefly, then slice with a sharp knife or pizza wheel.

Herbed Chicken Pizza

 Makes one 12-inch pizza

2 uncooked chicken breast halves

¾ cup balsamic vinegar dressing

1 cup mixed fresh herbs, chopped

1 recipe Chicago Deep-Dish Crust dough (Chapter 9)

1 tablespoon olive oil

2 cups chunky tomato sauce

2 cups shredded mozzarella cheese

Combine standbys like green onions, garlic, and parsley with fresh lemon thyme, purple basil, chervil, pineapple sage, and other fresh herbs to make this pizza special.

1. Place chicken breast halves in a resealable plastic bag. Whisk ½ cup of herb mixture into the vinegar dressing and pour dressing over the chicken. Seal bag and refrigerate for 6 hours or overnight.
2. Remove chicken from marinade and discard marinade. Grill or pan-sear chicken until cooked through. Thinly slice chicken breasts and toss with remaining ½ cup of mixed herbs.
3. Roll out circle of pie crust dough. Spread olive oil in 12-inch deep-dish pizza or pie pan. Press dough circle into pan and prick bottom a few times with a fork. Ladle 2 cups of tomato sauce into each pan, followed by ½ cup of mozzarella cheese.
4. Arrange herb-coated chicken slices over the cheese. Divide remaining 1½ cups of mozzarella over the chicken slices. Bake at 400°F until browned and bubbly, about 20 minutes.

About Marinades

Marinades tenderize tough protein fibers while adding flavor to the meat. The best marinades have a high acid content from vinegar or fruit juices, plus aromatic flavoring agents. Since marinades have come in contact with raw meats, drained marinade must be discarded or, if to be used as a sauce or baste, brought to a full boil to kill bacteria before using.

Mesquite-Smoked Chicken and Peppers Pizza

Makes one 12-inch pizza

1 recipe Pizza Crust for the Grill dough (see recipe to follow)

Cornmeal and flour for dusting

Vegetable oil

1½ tablespoon olive oil

½ cup tomato sauce

1⅔ cup mozzarella cheese

1 cup diced mesquite-smoked chicken

½ small red bell pepper, cored and cut in strips

½ small yellow or green bell pepper, cored and cut in strips

If you're handy with a smoker, by all means make your own smoked chicken in advance of making pizza. Otherwise, buy prepared smoked chicken or substitute grilled chicken. Use white or dark meat according to your preferences.

1. On a lightly floured board or on parchment, roll out 12-inch dough circle. Place circle of dough on a metal pizza peel or rimless baking sheet generously sprinkled with flour and cornmeal.
2. Prepare a gas or charcoal grill so that one area is hot while another side or corner is medium-hot. Add soaked mesquite chips to the coals or place in a wood chip container for gas grills. Brush the grill rack with vegetable oil. Slide the pizza onto the grill rack over the hot coals or heating element. Close the lid immediately and grill for 2 to 3 minutes or until pizza dough is cooked on the bottom and grill marks appear. Remove dough to peel or baking sheet, turning the grilled side up.
3. Brush the grilled pizza side with half the olive oil, then quickly spread half the pizza sauce. Cover the sauce with half the slices of mozzarella and half the slices of provolone. Top with 1 cup diced smoked chicken and half the pepper strips.
4. Carefully slide the pizza back onto the grill, placing it over the medium-hot area. Close grill cover and cook 3 minutes. Check to make sure crust isn't browning too quickly. If it is, move some coals to the opposite side of the grill or lower gas grill thermostat to reduce heat. Continue to cook for another 4 to 5 minutes or until crust is browned and cheese is melted and bubbly. Remove from heat, cool slightly, and serve. Repeat cooking process with second pizza.

PIZZA CRUST FOR THE GRILL

Makes crust for one 12-inch pizza

½ package active dry yeast

½ cup warm water, about 110°F

¼ teaspoon sugar

½ teaspoon salt

1¼ cup bread flour

¼ cup semolina flour

⅛ cup whole-wheat or rye flour

½ tablespoon olive oil

1. In a large measuring cup, dissolve yeast in water. Let stand 5 minutes or until bubbly. Combine sugar, salt, and all flours in the bowl of a mixer with a dough hook. Or, to mix by hand, place in a large bowl. Make a well in the flour mixture and pour in the water, followed by 1 tablespoon of oil.

2. Turn the mixer on low to blend, or begin stirring the flour into the liquid with a wooden spoon, a little at a time. When ingredients are well combined, turn the mixer on medium-low to knead for 5 minutes. If working dough by hand, turn the dough onto a well-floured work surface. Use a pressing motion with the heels of your hands to push and stretch the dough. Work dough until mixture is slightly shiny and not too sticky to the touch.

3. Oil dough and place in a bowl, covered, to rise for 1 hour. Punch the dough down, shape into a disk, and let rest for 30 minutes.

4. Grab dough by the edges, turning the disk a few inches at a time, allowing gravity to stretch the dough without tearing. Roll the dough into a crust shape or press into a pizza pan. Top as directed in recipe.

Practice, Practice

While it may seem like "everybody" is making grilled pizza, the truth is that the technique requires a bit of practice. If you'd like to start slowly, try grilling your pie indoors on an electric breakfast griddle or heavy stovetop grill pan. Cook the crust on both sides, turning once, then top and slide into the oven to finish cooking the toppings.

The $5 Takeout Cookbook

Chicken Parmesan Pizza

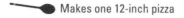 Makes one 12-inch pizza

$ Total Cost: $5.00

1 cup thinly sliced chicken cutlets

Salt and pepper to taste

½ cup granulated flour

2 eggs

¼ cup milk

1 cups Italian-style seasoned bread crumbs

¼ cup grated Parmesan cheese

Vegetable oil for frying

1 recipe Classic Crust dough (Chapter 9)

2 tablespoons olive oil

1 cup chunky tomato sauce

1¼ cups shredded mozzarella cheese

1. Salt and pepper veal, then lightly coat each slice with flour.
2. Whisk together eggs and milk. Pour bread crumbs and parmesan into a large plate or pie pan. Dip each chicken slice in egg mixture and coat lightly with seasoned bread crumbs mixture.
3. In a large skillet, pour oil to a depth of about 2 inches. Heat over medium-high heat until a drop of water sizzles in the oil. Fry chicken slices, a few at a time, until browned. Drain on paper towels.
4. Roll out circle of pie crust dough. Spread olive oil in 12-inch deep-dish pizza or pie pan. Press dough circle into pan and prick bottom a few times with a fork. Ladle 2 cups of tomato sauce into each pan, followed by ½ cup of mozzarella cheese.
5. Arrange fried chicken slices over the cheese, overlapping as necessary. Divide remaining mozzarella over the chicken slices. Bake at 400°F until browned and bubbly, about 20 minutes.

CHAPTER 11

MEATS

Italian Sausage and Mushroom Pizza

 Makes one 12-inch pizza

1 recipe Classic Crust dough (Chapter 9)

1 tablespoon cornmeal or 1 tablespoon olive oil

¾ cup tomato sauce

1½ cup shredded mozzarella cheese

½ pound hot or mild Italian sausage, browned and sliced diagonally

4 ounces white mushrooms, sliced

¼ teaspoon dried oregano

It's possible to buy five different brands of Italian sausage and get five different spice blends. Each purveyor follows its own recipe. Sample until you find one that suits you.

1. Roll or press pizza dough into 12-inch circle, slightly thicker at the edges than in the center. If using pizza pan, sprinkle the bottom with cornmeal or coat with olive oil and place dough in pan. If using a pizza stone, sprinkle with cornmeal and place stone in oven. Preheat oven to 400°F.

2. Spread ¾ cup sauce in the center of pizza, leaving edges bare.

3. Distribute 1½ cups mozzarella evenly over pizza, leaving one inch around the edges bare.

4. Arrange sausage slices evenly over cheese on pizza. Distribute mushrooms over pies, followed by a sprinkle of oregano.

5. If using a hot stone or tiles, use a well-floured pizza peel to carefully lift pizza from preparation surface and place on stone. Bake for 15 to 20 minutes or until the crust is lightly browned and cheese is melted.

6. Remove pizza from oven carefully (use peel if baking with a stone). Set aside to rest briefly before slicing.

To Sauté or Not to Sauté?

Fresh mushrooms are a mainstay pizza ingredient, appearing on both veggie and meat pies. White button mushrooms, thinly sliced, can be added to pizza raw and allowed to cook with the pizza. However, tougher varieties of mushrooms benefit from sautéing in advance of being added to pizza.

Meatball Pizza

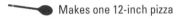

Makes one 12-inch pizza

$ Total Cost: $4.69

½ pound ground beef

½ egg

½ cup soft bread crumbs

½ tablespoon Worcestershire sauce

1 green onions, minced

⅛ cup fresh parsley leaves, minced

Salt and pepper to taste

1 recipe Pan Pizza Crust dough (Chapter 9)

1 tablespoon olive oil

1 cups chunky tomato sauce

1¾ cups shredded mozzarella cheese

1. In a large bowl, combine beef, egg, bread crumbs, Worcestershire sauce, green onions, and parsley. Add salt and pepper to taste. Work together with hands until well blended and ingredients have been evenly distributed in the meat. (If mixture seems dry, add a small amount of water or club soda to moisten.)
2. Roll the beef mixture into small meatballs, about 1 inch in diameter. Place meatballs on a baking sheet lined with non-stick foil. Bake at 350°F, turning occasionally, until meatballs are cooked through, about 15 minutes. Remove from oven.
3. Roll out circle of pie crust dough. Spread olive oil in 12-inch deep-dish pizza or pie pan. Press dough circle into pan and prick bottom a few times with a fork.
4. Ladle sauce into pan, followed by ½ cup of mozzarella cheese. Divide the meatballs evenly over sauce and cheese in each pan.
5. Divide remaining mozzarella over the pizza. Bake at 400°F until browned and bubbly, about 20 minutes. Let stand 5 minutes, then serve with forks.

Pepperoni Pizza

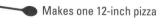 Makes one 12-inch pizza

1 recipe Classic Crust dough (Chapter 9)

1 tablespoon cornmeal or 1 tablespoon olive oil

¾ cup tomato sauce

½ cup shredded Parmesan cheese

1¼ cup shredded mozzarella cheese

4 ounces pepperoni, sliced

If you're a real pepperoni lover, feel free to increase the amount used on pizza. Buy freshly sliced pepperoni from a deli counter rather than prepackaged slices.

1. Roll or press pizza dough into 12-inch circle, slightly thicker at the edges than in the center. If using pizza pan, sprinkle the bottom with cornmeal or coat with olive oil and place dough in pan. If using a pizza stone, sprinkle with cornmeal and place stone in oven. Preheat oven to 400°F.
2. Spread ¾ cup sauce in the center of pizza, leaving one inch around the edges bare.
3. Sprinkle ½ cup Parmesan over the sauce on pizza. Distribute 1¼ cups mozzarella evenly over pizza, leaving edges bare. Distribute pepperoni slices evenly over pizza.
4. If baking on a hot stone or tiles, use a well-floured pizza peel to carefully lift one pizza from preparation surface and place on stone. Bake for 15 to 20 minutes or until the crust is lightly browned and cheese is melted.
5. Remove pizza from oven carefully (use peel if baking with a stone). Set aside to rest briefly before slicing.

Passion for Pepperoni

Pepperoni is by far America's favorite pizza topping, accounting for more than a third of pizza ordered. Pepperoni is a dry salami, made from beef, pork, veal, and spices. It's available in small or large diameter rolls and with varying levels of spiciness and moisture. Try several varieties to find your favorite.

Canadian Bacon and Pineapple Pizza

 Makes one 12-inch pizza

 Total Cost: $4.40

1 recipe Classic Crust dough (Chapter 9)

1 tablespoon cornmeal or 1 tablespoon olive oil

¾ cup tomato sauce

½ tablespoon honey

2 cups shredded mozzarella cheese

4 ounces Canadian bacon slices, quartered

½ cup diced green bell pepper

¾ cup quartered pineapple slices

¼ cup diced red onion

⅛ cup minced parsley

1. Roll or press pizza dough into 12-inch circle, slightly thicker at the edges than in the center. If using pizza pan, sprinkle the bottom with cornmeal or coat with olive oil and place dough in pan. If using a pizza stone, sprinkle with cornmeal and place stone in oven. Preheat oven to 400°F.
2. In a bowl, whisk together tomato sauce and honey. Spread half the sauce in the center of pizza, leaving one inch around the edges bare.
3. Distribute mozzarella evenly over pizza, leaving edges bare.
4. Dot pizza with half the Canadian bacon, followed by half the bell pepper and half the pineapple. Sprinkle onion and parsley over pizza.
5. If baking on a hot stone or tiles, use a well-floured pizza peel to carefully lift one pizza from preparation surface and place on stone. If using pizza pan, place first pizza in the center of the oven. Bake for 15 to 20 minutes or until the crust is lightly browned and toppings are bubbly.
6. Remove pizza from oven carefully (use peel if baking with a stone). Set aside to rest briefly before slicing.

Cheeseburger Pizza

Makes one 12-inch pizza

1 recipe Pan Pizza Crust dough
(Chapter 9)

1 tablespoon olive oil

1 cup tomato sauce

½ pound ground beef, cooked

1½ cup mozzarella cheese

⅓ cup crumbled bacon

½ cup chopped onion

Freshly ground black pepper

If you have a passion for mushroom burgers, just add a layer of sautéed white mushrooms over the ground beef.

1. Roll pizza dough into circle large enough to cover bottom and sides of 12-inch pizza or quiche pan. Spread a table-spoon of olive oil over the bottom of each pan, then press dough circle into the pan.
2. Ladle 1 cup sauce into pan and spread evenly over the crust. Top sauce with 1 cup mozzarella cheese, followed by ground beef.
3. Spread remaining mozzarella evenly over ground beef on pizza.
4. Dot cheese with crumbled bacon and onion. Add freshly ground black pepper to taste. Bake pan in a preheated oven at 400°F until crust has browned and cheese is bubbly, about 20 minutes.

Mini Pan Pies

Serve your guests their own individual pizza straight from the oven. Personal-size pizza pans can be purchased at kitchen supply stores, or you can simply use individual tart or crème brûlée pan. Bake at 400°F. Your pies should be nicely browned in 10 to 12 minutes. Serve the mini-pizza with a thatch of mixed greens tossed with a simple dressing and fresh fruit.

Beef Taco Pizza

Makes one 12-inch pizza

$ Total Cost: $4.65

1 recipe Classic Crust dough (Chapter 9)

1 tablespoon cornmeal or 1 tablespoon olive oil

¾ cup picante sauce

1 cup shredded Monterey jack cheese

½ cup cooked, taco-seasoned ground beef

¼ cup sliced green onion

2 cups shredded iceberg lettuce

1 cup diced tomatoes

½ cup sour cream

Taco-seasoned ground beef is available in ready-to-use tubs at supermarkets. Or make your own in 10 minutes with a packet of taco seasoning and ground beef. Just follow package directions.

1. Roll or press pizza dough into 12-inch circle, slightly thicker at the edges than in the center. If using pizza pan, sprinkle the bottom with cornmeal or coat with olive oil and place dough in pan. If using a pizza stone, sprinkle with cornmeal and place stone in oven. Preheat oven to 400°F.
2. Spread sauce in the center of pizza, leaving one inch around the edges bare.
3. Distribute 1 cup Monterey jack evenly over pizza, leaving edges bare.
4. Spread beef evenly over the cheese on pizza. Sprinkle sliced green onions over pizza.
5. If using a hot stone or tiles, use a well-floured pizza peel to carefully lift one pizza from preparation surface and place on stone. If using pizza pan, place first pizza in the center of the oven. Bake for 15 to 20 minutes or until the crust is lightly browned and toppings are bubbly.
6. Remove pizza from oven carefully (use peel if baking with a stone). Set aside to rest briefly before slicing. Just before serving, top pizza with shredded lettuce and tomatoes. Serve with sour cream.

Cheesesteak Pizza

 Makes 1 oblong pizza

$ Total Cost: $4.95

1 recipe Classic Crust dough (Chapter 9)	½ pound rib eye, sliced paper-thin
2 tablespoons olive oil	2 cloves garlic, minced
2 tablespoons cornmeal	½ cup parsley, minced
1 cup tomato sauce	Black pepper to taste
1 tablespoon butter	1½ cups shredded mozzarella cheese

Cheesesteak lovers fall into two camps: those who think cheesesteaks taste best with real cheese and those who prefer a melted cheese sauce drizzled on top. If you fall into the latter camp, just replace the mozzarella with diced processed cheese.

1. On a floured board, roll pizza dough into a rectangle. Coat an 11" × 16" oblong metal baking dish with olive oil and sprinkle with cornmeal. Press dough into the pan, spreading it to the corners.
2. Spread the sauce over the top of the dough.
3. In a large skillet or Dutch oven, heat butter over high heat. Add sliced steak and garlic and sauté 3 to 5 minutes until beef is cooked. Add parsley and black pepper and remove from heat. Arrange steak over the top of the pizza.
4. Spread mozzarella evenly over the top of the steak. Preheat oven to 400°F. Bake 20 to 25 minutes or until top is browned and bubbly. Cut into square slices with a sharp knife.

King of Steaks

At Pat's Steaks in South Philadelphia, steak sandwiches were created when the owners of a hot dog stand on the site decided to grill up steak sandwiches for their own supper. Regulars got a whiff and wanted the steaks too. The next day, steak sandwiches were all the rage. It took a few more years for the cheese to be added.

Carnivore's Delight

 Makes one 12-inch pizza

1 recipe Chicago Deep-Dish Crust dough (Chapter 9)

1¼ cups mozzarella cheese

½ cup chunky tomato sauce

¼ pound ground beef, browned

⅛ pound bulk sausage, browned

¼ pound finely diced pepperoni

This hearty pizza isn't for the faint of heart. Serve it on a cold day with forks and plenty of napkins.

1. Coat 12-inch deep-dish pizza or pie pan with olive oil. Divide dough and press into pan, making sure dough goes all the way up the sides of the pan. Preheat oven to 450°F.
2. Sprinkle mozzarella over the crust of pizza, using about half the mozzarella. Pour ¼ cup sauce in the center of pizza and spread evenly over the mozzarella. Sprinkle the meats, in the order listed, evenly over the sauce.
3. Sprinkle remaining mozzarella evenly over the meats. Spread remaining sauce over the cheese layer, dividing evenly over the two pizza.
4. Reduce heat to 400°F and bake pizza for 20 to 25 minutes or until crust is light brown and centers are browned and bubbly.

Sausage Savvy

Most sausages labeled Italian sausage or breakfast sausages and some chorizos are fresh sausages, which means they're very perishable and must be cooked thoroughly before using. Never add uncooked fresh sausage to pizza. Even if the pizza is in the oven long enough to cook the sausage, you'll wind up with plenty of unwanted grease on your pie.

The $5 Takeout Cookbook

Matchstick Beef and Caramelized Onion Pizza

 Makes one 12-inch pizza

$ Total Cost: $4.38

1 tablespoon vegetable oil

1 clove garlic, pressed

½ tablespoon Worcestershire sauce

½ tablespoon prepared mustard

½ tablespoon lemon juice

1 tablespoon ketchup

¼ teaspoon cumin

¼ pound roasted beef, cut into matchstick pieces

1 large sweet onions, thinly sliced

1½ tablespoon butter

¼ teaspoon sugar

1 recipe Classic Crust dough (Chapter 9)

1 tablespoon olive oil

1 tablespoon cornmeal

½ cup Horseradish Sauce (see recipe to follow)

1 cup shredded mozzarella cheese

This sweet-and-savory pie gets a spicy kick from the Horseradish Sauce. Leftover roast beef works perfectly in this dish.

1. In a large bowl, combine oil, garlic, Worcestershire sauce, mustard, lemon juice, ketchup, and cumin. Add matchstick beef and toss well to coat. Set aside.
2. In a large skillet or Dutch oven, combine onions, butter, and sugar. Cook over medium heat, stirring often, until onions reach a uniform deep brown color.
3. Roll or press pizza dough into thin 12-inch circle, slightly thicker at the edges than in the center. Divide 1 tablespoon olive oil over the bottom of a pizza pan or large quiche pan. Sprinkle cornmeal over the oil.
4. Preheat oven to 400°F. Spread Horseradish Sauce over pizza, leaving edges bare. Spread cheese evenly over the sauce.
5. Top cheese on pizza with a generous tangle of caramelized onions, followed by seasoned matchstick beef.
6. Place pizza in the oven and bake until shredded cheese has melted and crust darken slightly, about 10 to 12 minutes. Let pizza rest briefly, then slice with a sharp knife or pizza wheel. If oven won't accommodate both pan easily, bake pizza one at a time.

HORSERADISH SAUCE

 Makes 1 cup

⅔ tablespoons butter

1⅓ cloves garlic, minced

1⅓ tablespoon finely grated fresh horseradish

⅓ cup heavy cream

⅓ cup softened cream cheese

⅓ cup shredded Parmesan cheese

Salt and freshly ground black pepper to taste

Horseradish root starts losing pungency once it is grated and exposed to air. For peak flavor, grate horseradish just before adding to the sauce.

1. In a heavy saucepan over medium heat, melt butter and sauté garlic briefly. Add horseradish, cream, cream cheese, and Parmesan. Whisk until all ingredients are blended and cheese has melted.
2. Cook sauce a few minutes until thick and bubbly. Add salt and pepper to taste. Remove from heat and cool slightly before using in recipes.

Gyro Pizza

 Makes one 12-inch pizza

1 recipe Classic Crust dough (Chapter 9)

1 tablespoon cornmeal or 2 tablespoons olive oil

⅓ cup whole-milk ricotta cheese

½ tablespoon plain yogurt

1 green onions, minced

1 clove garlic, pressed

⅛ cup minced parsley

Black pepper to taste

1⅓ cup shredded mozzarella cheese

½ cup diced tomatoes

3 ounces gyro meat, chopped

Gyro meat is a dense loaf of minced and spiced pork, lamb, or beef that's spit-roasted. Many supermarkets carry it in the freezer section. A few carry fresh gyro meat in the deli section.

1. Roll or press pizza dough into 12-inch circle, slightly thicker at the edges than in the center. If using pizza pan, sprinkle the bottom with cornmeal or coat with olive oil and place dough in pan. If using a pizza stone, sprinkle with cornmeal and place stone in oven. Preheat oven to 400°F.
2. Combine ricotta with yogurt, green onion, garlic, and parsley. Add black pepper to taste. Spread ricotta mixture over pizza, leaving edges bare. Sprinkle mozzarella over pizza, followed by tomatoes and gyro meat.
3. If baking on a hot stone or tiles, use a well-floured pizza peel to carefully lift pizza from preparation surface and place on stone. If using pizza pan, place pizza in the center of the oven. Bake for 15 to 20 minutes or until the crust is lightly browned and toppings are bubbly.
4. Remove pizza from oven carefully (use peel if baking with a stone). Set aside to rest briefly before slicing.

Szechwan Shredded Pork Pizza

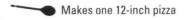 Makes one 12-inch pizza

1 tablespoon dark sesame oil

½ tablespoon vegetable oil

1 clove garlic, minced

½ teaspoon minced fresh ginger

¼ cup chopped water chestnuts

¼ cup matchstick-sliced mushrooms

¾ green onion, minced

1 cup shredded roasted pork shoulder

¼ cup soy sauce

½ tablespoon hot chili paste

½ tablespoon maple syrup

1 recipe Classic Crust dough (Chapter 9)

1 tablespoon cornmeal or 1 tablespoon oil

½ cup soy sauce

½ cup shredded mozzarella cheese

This pizza can easily go cheeseless for those who prefer a dairy-free pie. Inexpensive cuts of slow-cooked pork shred easily and work best in this recipe.

1. In a large, flat-bottomed wok over high heat, combine sesame and vegetable oils, garlic, and ginger. Stir-fry for 10 seconds before adding water chestnuts, mushrooms, bamboo shoots, and green onion. Stir-fry until vegetables are crisp-tender, about 5 minutes. Reduce heat and add pork. Combine soy sauce, hot chili paste, and syrup. Add to wok and simmer just until most liquid has evaporated, stirring often.
2. Roll or press pizza dough into very thin 12-inch circle, slightly thicker at the edges than in the center. If using pizza pan, sprinkle the bottom with cornmeal or coat with oil and place dough in pan. If using a pizza stone, sprinkle with cornmeal and place rolled dough directly on stone.
3. Paint each crust with soy sauce. Divide pork mixture evenly over each crust and sprinkle with mozzarella, if desired. Place pizza in the oven at 425°F. Bake 10 to 12 minutes or until crust is browned. Let pizza rest briefly, then slice with a sharp knife or pizza wheel.

Roast Pork and Spinach Pizza

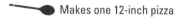 Makes one 12-inch pizza

1 recipe Classic Crust dough (Chapter 9)

1 tablespoon cornmeal or 1 tablespoon olive oil

¾ cup tomato sauce

1 cup shredded mozzarella cheese

¾ cup spinach, cleaned and lightly steamed

¼ pound roasted pork tenderloin, thinly sliced

¼ cup finely chopped sundried tomatoes

Fresh spinach has a wonderful, aromatic flavor. But it also harbors a lot of water that can make pizza and other dishes soggy. Be sure to squeeze liquid from spinach before adding to other dishes.

1. Roll or press pizza dough into 12-inch circle, slightly thicker at the edges than in the center. If using pizza pan, sprinkle the bottom with cornmeal or coat with olive oil and place dough in pan. If using a pizza stone, sprinkle with cornmeal and place stone in oven. Preheat oven to 400°F.
2. Spread ¾ cup sauce in the center of pizza, leaving edges bare.
3. In a large bowl, combine all the cheeses and toss gently to mix. Sprinkle half the cheese blend over the sauce on pizza, leaving edges bare.
4. Press as much water as possible from steamed spinach. Coarsely chop spinach and distribute evenly over cheese on pizza. Top cheese and spinach with sliced pork. Sprinkle with sun-dried tomatoes.
5. If baking with a hot stone or tiles, use a well-floured pizza peel to carefully lift one pizza from preparation surface and place on stone. Bake for 15 to 20 minutes or until the crust is lightly browned and cheese is melted.
6. Remove pizza from oven carefully (use peel if baking with a stone). Set aside to rest briefly before slicing.

Hot Italian Sausage and Fennel Pizza

 Makes 1 oblong pizza

1 recipe Classic Crust dough (Chapter 9)

2 tablespoons olive oil

2 tablespoons cornmeal

¾ cup tomato sauce

¼ pound bulk hot Italian sausage, browned

1 tablespoon butter

1 cup sliced fennel bulb

2 cloves garlic, minced

½ cup parsley, minced

Black pepper to taste

1 cup shredded mozzarella cheese

This thick pie travels well and still tastes great at room temperature. Bring it to your next potluck lunch or dinner.

1. On a floured board, roll pizza dough into a rectangle. Coat an 11" × 16" oblong metal baking dish with olive oil and sprinkle with cornmeal. Press dough into pan, spreading it to the corners.
2. Spread sauce over the top of the dough, followed by browned hot sausage.
3. In a large skillet or Dutch oven, heat butter over medium-high heat. Add fennel, mushrooms, and garlic and sauté 3 minutes. Add parsley and remove from heat. Spread mixture evenly over pizza. Add black pepper to taste.
4. Spread mozzarella evenly over the top of the sausage and vegetables. Preheat oven to 400°F. Bake 20 to 25 minutes or until top is browned and bubbly. Cut into square slices with a sharp knife.

CHAPTER 12

CALZONES AND PIZZA TURNOVERS

Feta, Olive, and Tomato Calzones

 Makes three 8-inch calzones

1 recipe Classic Crust dough (Chapter 9)

½ cup Garlic and Oil Sauce (see recipe to follow)

½ cup chopped kalamata olives

1 teaspoon dried oregano

1 cup diced feta cheese

1 cup grape tomatoes, halved

¼ cup shredded mozzarella cheese

Black pepper to taste

3 tablespoons cornmeal

The feta cheese and olives will probably make this dish salty enough without adding extra salt.

1. Separate dough into three pieces. Place segments on a heavily floured work surface and roll each one into an 8-inch circle. Spread one-third of the sauce over each circle.
2. Combine olives, oregano, feta cheese, and tomatoes. Spoon one-third of the mixture onto half of each dough circle, leaving 1 inch around the edges bare. Sprinkle fillings with one-third of the pine nuts and one-third of the mozzarella cheese. Season with black pepper to taste.
3. Fold dough over the filling to form a crescent. Press dough edges together, brushing edges with a little water if necessary. Sprinkle cornmeal over a baking sheet or pizza tiles and place calzones on the cornmeal. Cover with a damp towel and let stand 1 hour.
4. With a sharp knife, cut two or three slits in the tops of the calzones. Bake at 375°F for 20 to 25 minutes. Remove from oven and let stand a few minutes before serving.

GARLIC AND OIL SAUCE

 Makes 1 cup

$ Total Cost: $2.81

1 cup extra virgin olive oil

10 cloves garlic, minced

½ tablespoon minced fresh parsley

¼ teaspoon red pepper flakes

Although this sauce is super-simple, care must be taken not to burn the garlic. Burnt garlic will make the sauce bitter.

1. In a saucepan or skillet, warm the olive oil over medium-low heat. Add garlic, parsley, and red pepper flakes. Cook, stirring often, for 4 to 5 minutes or until garlic has softened.

2. Remove from heat and cool slightly before using in recipes. Excess sauce can be tossed with pasta and Parmesan or refrigerated for later use.

Great Garlic

Garlic has been cultivated around the globe since ancient times, with a few dried bulbs even turning up in the tomb of King Tutankhamen. Although some find its pungent aroma disagreeable, most of the world's notable cuisines freely incorporate this onion-cousin. Americans each eat more than three pounds of garlic annually. Sulphur compounds give raw garlic its strong bite, but as garlic cooks the flavor becomes mellow, almost sweet. Garlic has antibiotic properties, as well as disease-fighting flavanoids.

Hot Pastrami Stromboli

 Makes one 16-inch roll

 Total Cost: $4.34

1 recipe Classic Crust dough (Chapter 9)

2 tablespoons olive oil

½ pound sliced pastrami

2 cups shredded mozzarella cheese

Black pepper to taste

2 tablespoons cornmeal

Hot mustard or pizza sauce for dipping (optional)

Cooks vary on whether stromboli should be a hollow tube of dough filled with meats and cheese, or a roll that yields goody-filled spiral slices. This version calls for a roll technique, making it easy to serve at parties.

1. On a floured surface, roll dough into a 9" × 16" rectangle. Brush liberally with olive oil, then cover dough with pastrami slices. Sprinkle mozzarella over the top, then sprinkle with black pepper.
2. Starting from a long side of the dough, lift the edge and begin rolling the dough tightly, jelly-roll fashion, being careful to encase the filling with each turn.
3. Sprinkle a baking sheet with cornmeal and place the roll on the sheet. Cover and let stand 1 hour. Bake at 375°F for 20 to 25 minutes or until nicely browned. Let stand a few minutes, then slice crosswise and serve with mustard or pizza sauce for dipping.

Try a Reuben

For an Octoberfest feast, make this stromboli with a layer of well-drained sauerkraut and a brush of Thousand Island dressing. Stick with the pastrami or go for lean slices of corned beef. Serve your Reuben stromboli in 1-inch slices as a nosh to go with mugs of whatever beer or ale you're serving.

Three-Sausage Calzones

 Makes three 8-inch calzones

$ Total Cost: $4.81

1 recipe Classic Crust dough (Chapter 9)

1 cup tomato sauce

¼ cup bulk Italian sausage, browned and drained

¼ cup diced andouille sausage

¼ cup diced kielbasa sausage

1⅓ cups shredded mozzarella cheese

Salt and black pepper to taste

3 tablespoons cornmeal

Fresh Italian sausage gives these calzones a hint of sweetness and fennel flavoring, while the andouille and kielbasa offer spicy and smoky tastes.

1. Separate dough into three pieces. Place segments on a heavily floured work surface and roll each one into an 8-inch circle. Brush each circle with tomato sauce.
2. Spread 1 cup of the mozzarella onto half of each dough circle, leaving one inch around the edges bare. Combine the three sausages in a bowl. Distribute one-third of the sausage mixture over the mozzarella on each calzone. Season with salt and black pepper to taste.
3. Fold dough over the filling to form a crescent. Press dough edges together, brushing edges with a little water if necessary. Sprinkle cornmeal over a baking sheet or pizza tiles and place calzones on the cornmeal. Cover with a damp towel and let stand 1 hour.
4. With a sharp knife, cut two or three slits in the tops of the calzones. Bake at 375°F for 20 to 25 minutes. Remove from oven and let stand a few minutes before serving.

Served Fresh, Smoked, or Cured

Europeans brought sausages to the New World in the fifteenth century. Smoked or salted and cured sausages— rich with bacteria-retarding fats—were a way of preserving meats of all varieties. Most farm families had their own recipes for sausage, and sausage vendors did a brisk business selling to ships going out to sea. Fresh sausage, which was seasoned but not yet dried or smoked, was a delicacy and one of the treats of the sausage kitchen.

Pepperoni Roll

Makes one 16-inch roll

1 recipe Classic Crust dough
  (Chapter 9)

1 tablespoon olive oil

1¼ cup sliced pepperoni

1½ cups shredded mozzarella
  cheese

Black pepper to taste

2 tablespoons cornmeal

This is a favorite Italian trattoria and bakery snack along the Eastern Seaboard. Some cooks make a distinctive roll, while others prepare something more akin to pepperoni bread.

1. On a floured surface, roll dough into a 9" × 16" rectangle. Brush liberally with olive oil, then cover dough with pepperoni slices. Sprinkle mozzarella over the top, then sprinkle with black pepper.
2. Starting from a long side of the dough, lift the edge and begin rolling the dough tightly, jelly-roll fashion, being careful to encase the filling with each turn.
3. Sprinkle a baking sheet with cornmeal and place the roll on the sheet. Cover and let stand 1 hour. Bake at 375°F for 20 to 25 minutes or until nicely browned. Let stand a few minutes, then slice crosswise and serve.

Zucchini and Tomato Turnovers

 Makes three 8-inch turnovers

1 recipe Classic Crust dough (Chapter 9)

½ cup tomato sauce

¾ cup ricotta cheese

¼ cup minced fresh basil

2 cloves garlic, minced

2 cups shredded zucchini

1⅓ cups diced tomatoes

2 cups shredded mozzarella

Salt and black pepper to taste

3 tablespoons cornmeal

Drain tomatoes for a few minutes and blot excess moisture from zucchini before combining ingredients in this recipe.

1. Separate dough into three pieces. Place segments on a heavily floured work surface and roll each one into an 8-inch circle. Spread one-third of the sauce over each circle.

2. Combine ricotta, basil, garlic, zucchini, and tomatoes. Spread one-third of the mixture onto half of each dough circle, leaving 1 inch around the edges bare. Distribute mozzarella cheese over filling on each turnover. Season with salt and black pepper to taste.

3. Fold dough over the filling to form a crescent. Press dough edges together, brushing edges with a little water if necessary. Sprinkle cornmeal over a baking sheet or pizza tiles and place calzones on the cornmeal. Cover with a damp towel and let stand 1 hour.

4. With a sharp knife, cut two or three slits in the tops of the calzones. Bake at 375°F for 20 to 25 minutes. Remove from oven and let stand a few minutes before serving.

Chili-Beef Calzones

 Makes three 8-inch calzones

1 recipe Classic Crust dough
(Chapter 9)

½ cup picante sauce

⅔ cup cooked shredded beef
brisket

1 cup drained black beans

1 (15-ounce) can chili-
seasoned tomato sauce

¼ cup minced fresh cilantro

2 cloves garlic, minced

2 green onions, minced

½ jalapeño pepper, minced

½ teaspoon cumin

Salt and black pepper to taste

2 cups shredded mozzarella
cheese

3 tablespoons cornmeal

Your favorite leftover chili can substitute for the chili-bean
mixture in this dish.

1. Separate dough into three pieces. Place segments on a
   heavily floured work surface and roll each one into an 8-inch
   circle. Spread one-third of the Picante Sauce over each
   circle.
2. In a large bowl, combine beef, beans, chili sauce, cilantro,
   garlic, green onions, jalapeño pepper, cumin, salt, and pepper. Spoon one-third of the mixture over half of each dough
   circle, leaving 1 inch around the edges bare. Distribute
   cheese over the filling on each calzone.
3. Fold dough over the filling to form a crescent. Press dough
   edges together, brushing edges with a little water if necessary. Sprinkle cornmeal over a baking sheet or pizza tiles
   and place calzones on the cornmeal. Cover with a damp
   towel and let stand 1 hour.
4. With a sharp knife, cut two or three slits in the tops of the
   calzones. Bake at 375°F for 20 to 25 minutes. Remove from
   oven and let stand a few minutes before serving.

The $5 Takeout Cookbook

PART FOUR
CHINESE

What is it that makes Chinese food so special? It's not the exotic vegetables and seasonings—a skilled chef can prepare a meal that epitomizes the best of Chinese cooking using only native ingredients. It's not the equipment, either. Many tasty stir-fries have been born in a frying pan instead of a wok.

The true secret to Chinese cuisine lies in a harmonious blending of flavors, textures, and colors. Take Sweet-and-Sour Pork, for example. The sweet and sour flavors balance each other nicely, and the reddish sauce provides a nice contrast to the pineapple and green bell peppers.

So, why aren't more people stir-frying noodles and boiling dumplings? A common misconception is that it takes a skilled chef working with state-of-the-art equipment to prepare good Chinese food. Fortunately, that's not true. Stir-frying, steaming, and deep-frying—the three primary Chinese cooking techniques—are all easily mastered with practice. Now with this book, you no longer need to rely on your favorite Chinese restaurant for all your takeout favorites, such as Mu Shu Pork and Sesame Chicken, because you too can easily whip up these delectable dishes!

CHAPTER 13

BEEF

Basic Beef Stir-Fry

 Serves 2–4

½ pound beef

2 teaspoons soy sauce

1 teaspoon cornstarch

¼ teaspoon baking soda

1 tablespoon vegetable oil

2 tablespoons oil for stir-frying

1 clove garlic, smashed

1 tablespoon Chinese rice
   wine or dry sherry

½ teaspoon sugar

This is a good basic recipe for marinating and stir-frying beef that you can adapt according to your tastes and the ingredients you have on hand.

1. Cut the beef across the grain into thin strips. Add the soy sauce, cornstarch, and baking soda to the meat, in that order. Use your hands to mix in the cornstarch and baking soda. Marinate the meat for 30 minutes, add the vegetable oil, and marinate for another 30 minutes.
2. Add oil to a preheated wok or skillet. When oil is hot, add the garlic and stir-fry briefly until aromatic. Add the beef, laying it flat on the wok. Let the meat cook for a minute, turn over and brown on the other side, and then begin stir-frying. When it is nearly cooked through, add the rice wine and sugar. When the meat is cooked, remove from the wok and drain on paper towels.

Searing Meat

While stir-frying is normally a hands-on process, when cooking meat it's best to give the spatula a brief rest. Lay the meat out flat in the wok and brown for about 30 seconds before stir-frying.

Mongolian Beef with Vegetables

 Serves 2

$ Total Cost: $4.15

½ pound sirloin or flank steak

1 egg white

Pinch of salt

¾ teaspoon sesame oil, divided

½ tablespoon cornstarch

¾ tablespoon oil

1 green onions

1 garlic clove, minced

¼ teaspoon chili sauce

½ can baby corn, rinsed and drained

½ tablespoon Chinese rice wine or dry sherry

1 tablespoon hoisin sauce

½ tablespoon dark soy sauce

¼ teaspoon sugar

¾ teaspoon cornstarch

1 tablespoon water

½ cup oil for frying beef

This northern Chinese favorite makes a complete meal when served with rice. For a more authentic dish, use bamboo shoots instead of baby corn.

1. Slice the beef across the grain into thin strips. Add the egg white, salt, ½ teaspoon sesame oil, and cornstarch to the beef, adding the cornstarch last. Marinate the beef for 30 minutes. Add ¾ tablespoon oil and marinate for another thirty minutes.
2. While beef is marinating, cut the green onions into thirds on the diagonal.
3. Add 1 cup oil to a preheated wok or skillet. When oil is hot, carefully slide the beef into the wok, a few pieces at a time. Fry the beef until it changes color. Remove from the wok with a slotted spoon and drain on paper towels.
4. Remove all but 2 tablespoons of oil. When oil is hot, add the garlic and chili sauce. Stir-fry briefly until the garlic is aromatic. Add the baby corn.
5. Add the beef back into the wok. Add the rice wine, hoisin sauce, dark soy sauce, and sugar. Mix the cornstarch and water, and add to the middle of the wok, stirring vigorously to thicken. Mix all the ingredients together thoroughly. Stir in the green onion. Drizzle with ⅓ tablespoon sesame oil and serve hot.

Beef with Snow Peas

Serves 2–4

¾ pound beef flank steak

2 teaspoons soy sauce

1 teaspoon cornstarch

¼ teaspoon baking soda

½ cup snow peas

1 cup mung bean sprouts

1 tablespoon dark soy sauce

1 tablespoon oyster sauce

1 tablespoon Chinese rice wine or dry sherry

1 teaspoon sugar

¼ teaspoon sesame oil

2 tablespoons water

3 tablespoons oil for stir-frying

2 garlic cloves, minced

1. Cut the beef across the grain into thin strips about 2 inches long. Add the soy sauce, cornstarch, and baking soda. Marinate the beef for 30 minutes.
2. Trim the snow peas. Blanch the bean sprouts and snow peas by plunging them briefly into boiling water. Drain well.
3. In a small bowl, combine the dark soy sauce, oyster sauce, rice wine, sugar, sesame oil, and water and set aside.
4. Add 2 tablespoons oil to a preheated wok or skillet. When oil is hot, add the beef and stir-fry until it changes color. Remove from the wok and drain on paper towels.
5. Add another tablespoon of oil to the wok. When oil is hot, add the garlic and stir-fry briefly until aromatic. Add the snow peas and bean sprouts and stir-fry briefly. Add the sauce in the middle of the wok and bring to a boil. Mix with the vegetables. Add the beef. Add 1–2 more tablespoons water if desired. Mix everything together and serve hot.

Beef and Bean Sprouts in Black Bean Sauce

 Serves 2–4

½ pound beef steak

2 teaspoons soy sauce

¼ teaspoon salt

½ teaspoon sugar

1 teaspoon cornstarch

¼ teaspoon baking soda

1 cup mung bean sprouts

1 teaspoon fermented black beans

¼ teaspoon chili paste

½ cup chicken stock or broth

1 tablespoon dark soy sauce

1 teaspoon sugar

1 teaspoon red rice vinegar

3 tablespoons oil for stir-frying

1 garlic clove, minced

This dish can also be made with green jalapeño peppers—chop 3 jalapeño peppers, remove the seeds, and stir-fry with the chili paste.

1. Cut the beef across the grain into thin strips about 2 inches long. Add the soy sauce, salt, sugar, cornstarch, and baking soda. Marinate the beef for 30 minutes.
2. Blanch the bean sprouts by plunging very briefly into boiling water. Drain thoroughly. Soak the black beans, mash, and mix with the chili paste.
3. Mix together the chicken broth, dark soy sauce, and sugar.
4. Add 2 tablespoons oil to a preheated wok or skillet. When oil is hot, add the beef and stir-fry until it changes color and is nearly cooked through. Remove from the wok and drain on paper towels.
5. Add 1 tablespoon oil to the wok. When oil is hot, add the garlic and chili paste mixture. Stir-fry briefly until aromatic. Add the bean sprouts. Stir-fry briefly, and then add the red rice vinegar.
6. Add the sauce in the middle of the wok and bring to a boil. Add the beef. Simmer until everything is cooked through.

Mu Shu Beef

Serves 2–3

½ pound beef

½ cup water

1 tablespoon dark soy sauce

1 tablespoon plus 1 teaspoon
hoisin sauce

1 teaspoon sugar

1 teaspoon oyster sauce

¼ teaspoon sesame oil

2 eggs, lightly beaten

¼ teaspoon salt

3–4 tablespoons oil for
stir-frying

1 slice ginger, minced

½ cup mung bean sprouts,
rinsed and drained

For a more flavorful dish, try marinating the beef in oyster sauce, sugar, and cornstarch, adding the cornstarch last.

1. Cut the beef into thin slices. Marinate if desired.
2. Combine the water, dark soy sauce, hoisin sauce, sugar, oyster sauce, and sesame oil, and set aside.
3. Mix the eggs with ¼ teaspoon salt. Add 1 tablespoon oil to a preheated wok or skillet. When oil is hot, scramble the eggs and remove from the wok.
4. Add 2 more tablespoons oil. When oil is hot, add the beef and stir-fry until it changes color and is nearly cooked through. Remove from the wok and set aside.
5. Add more oil if necessary. Add the ginger and stir-fry briefly until aromatic. Add the bean sprouts. Add the sauce and bring to a boil. Add the beef and the scrambled egg. Mix everything together and serve hot.

Spicy Steamed Beef

 Serves 2

½ pound sirloin or flank steak

½ tablespoon soy sauce

¼ teaspoon baking soda

1 tablespoon dark soy sauce

¼ teaspoon sugar

⅛ teaspoon dried crushed chili flakes

½ tablespoon dried orange peel

½ tablespoon Szechwan Salt and Pepper Mix (Chapter 14)

This dish tastes good served hot or cold. For a tasty appetizer, deep-fry the steamed beef twice in a flour, cornstarch, and egg batter. See Spicy Orange Beef (recipe to follow) for an example of this technique.

1. Cut the beef across the grain into thin slices about 1½ inches long. Add the soy sauce and baking soda, using your fingers to mix it in the baking soda. Marinate the beef for 30 minutes.
2. Combine the dark soy sauce, sugar, and crushed chili flakes. Cut the dried orange peel into thin slices.
3. Prepare the wok for steaming. Place the beef on a heatproof plate on a bamboo steamer. Rub the roasted peppercorn mixture over the beef. Brush on half of the sauce. Place the orange peel slices around the beef.
4. Steam the beef for 20 minutes or until it is cooked through. Brush on the remainder of the sauce during steaming.

Make Your Own Orange Peel

To make dried orange peel, remove the skin from an orange. Use a paring knife to remove the white pith inside. Leave the peel to dry in the sun or dry quickly by placing in a previously warmed oven. Remove the peel before it hardens.

The $5 Takeout Cookbook

Spicy Orange Beef

Serves 2–3

½ pound flank steak

2–3 cups oil for frying

1 garlic clove, minced

1½ slices ginger, minced

½ dried chili

2 tablespoons soy sauce

1 teaspoon Chinese rice wine or dry sherry

1 teaspoon sugar

¼ teaspoon chili paste

1 medium eggs

1½ tablespoon flour

1 tablespoon cornstarch

½ teaspoon dried orange peel or 1 small piece dried tangerine peel

This recipe shows fiery Szechwan cuisine at its finest—for a less spicy dish, leave out the dried chili.

1. Cut the beef across the grain into thin slices about 2 inches in length. Remove the seeds from the chili and chop.
2. Combine the soy sauce, rice wine, sugar, and chili paste, and set aside.
3. Beat the eggs and mix with the flour and cornstarch into a batter. Coat the beef slices with the batter, using your fingers.
4. Heat 2 to 3 cups of oil to 350°F. When oil is hot, add a few pieces of beef into the hot oil and deep-fry until they turn light brown. Remove with a slotted spoon and drain on paper towels. Continue with the rest of the beef.
5. Raise the oil temperature to 400°F. Deep-fry the beef pieces a second time, until they turn brown and crispy. Remove and drain.
6. Remove all but 2 tablespoons of oil from the wok or add 2 tablespoons oil to a second wok or skillet. Add the garlic, ginger, chili, and orange peel. Stir-fry until aromatic. Add the sauce and bring to a boil. Add the beef. Mix everything through and serve hot.

Orange Peel Cold Cure

Have a cold? Why not try an orange peel cure? For centuries, Chinese medical practitioners have recommended dried orange peel to treat everything from colds to insomnia. Whatever their medicinal value, there is no doubt that the peel contains more vitamin C than any other part of the orange.

Stir-Fried Orange Beef

Serves 2

1 teaspoon Chinese rice wine or dry sherry, divided

¼ teaspoon baking soda

½ pound round steak, shredded

1 tablespoon dried orange peel

½ green onion

1 tablespoon soy sauce

½ teaspoon sugar

⅛ teaspoon chili paste

1½ tablespoons oil for stir-frying

1 slices ginger, minced

½ clove garlic, minced

Leftovers can be used to make sandwiches—purée the beef with a bit of water and spread on buttered bread.

1. Add ½ teaspoon rice wine and baking soda, using your fingers to add the baking soda, to the beef. Marinate the beef for 30 minutes.
2. Cut the dried orange peel into thin slices. Cut the green onion into 1½-inch slices on the diagonal.
3. Combine the soy sauce, sugar, chili paste, and ½ teaspoon rice wine. Set aside.
4. Add 1 tablespoon oil to a preheated wok or skillet. When oil is hot, add the beef. Stir-fry until it is nearly cooked through. Remove from the wok and drain on paper towels.
5. Add ½ tablespoon oil. Add the ginger, garlic, green onion, and dried orange peel. Stir-fry until the orange peel is aromatic. Add the sauce in the middle and bring to a boil. Add the beef back in. Mix everything and stir-fry until the beef is cooked through, and serve hot.

Beef Satay

Serves 3

Total Cost: $1.44

¼ pound beef sirloin steak

⅛ cup dark soy sauce

⅛ teaspoon chili paste

½ tablespoon hoisin sauce

½ teaspoon sugar

½ teaspoon orange marmalade

½ clove garlic, minced

½ slice ginger, minced

For an authentic touch, thread the meat onto bamboo skewers that have been soaked in cold water for 30 minutes (to ensure that they don't burn).

1. Cut the beef across the grain into very thin strips, about 1 inch long.
2. Combine the remaining ingredients. Marinate the beef in the refrigerator overnight or for at least 2 hours. Drain the beef, reserving the marinade.
3. Thread at least 2 slices of the marinated beef onto each skewer, weaving them in and out like an accordion. Brush with the reserved marinade.
4. Grill the beef on both sides. Serve with Hoisin Satay Sauce (see recipe to follow).

HOISIN SATAY SAUCE

Yields ⅓ cup

Total Cost: $1.83

3 tablespoons hoisin sauce

2 teaspoons dark soy sauce

1 teaspoon rice vinegar

1 teaspoon orange marmalade

Up to ¼ teaspoon cayenne pepper flakes

1 clove garlic, chopped

¼ cup peanuts, crushed

Orange marmalade lends flavor to a traditional hoisin-based sauce in this fusion recipe. For a different taste, substitute 1 tablespoon of honey.

Combine all the ingredients.

Mongolian Beef with Rice Noodles

 Serves 2

$ Total Cost: $4.95

½ pound round steak

1 tablespoon dark soy sauce, divided

½ tablespoon Chinese rice wine or dry sherry

½ teaspoon sesame oil

½ tablespoon cornstarch

3 ounces rice vermicelli noodles

½ bunch leeks

½ tablespoon hoisin sauce

¼ teaspoon sugar

¼ teaspoon chili sauce

1 garlic clove, minced

¾ teaspoon cornstarch

1 tablespoon water

¾ cup oil for frying

Leeks are a popular vegetable in northern China, where cooks rely on hardy vegetables that can survive cold winters and a short growing season.

1. Slice the beef across the grain into thin slices. Add dark soy sauce, sherry, sesame oil, and cornstarch, adding the cornstarch last. Marinate the beef for 30 minutes. Soak the rice vermicelli in hot water for 15–20 minutes to soften. Drain thoroughly.
2. Wash the leek bunch, and cut into slices about 1½-inches long. Mix together the hoisin sauce, sugar, chili sauce, and 1 tablespoon dark soy sauce. Set aside.
3. Heat ¾ cup oil to 350°F in a preheated wok. When the oil is hot, add the rice vermicelli. Deep-fry until they puff up and turn crispy. Remove and drain on paper towels.
4. Remove all but 2 tablespoons oil. When oil is hot, add the garlic and stir-fry until aromatic. Add the beef and stir-fry until it changes color and is nearly cooked through. Remove and drain on paper towels.
5. Add more oil, if necessary. Add the leeks to the wok. Stir-fry for about 1 minute. Add the sauce to the middle of the wok. Mix the cornstarch and water and add to the sauce, stirring to thicken. Bring to a boil. Add the beef back into the wok and mix all the ingredients together. Serve over the rice noodles.

Basic Red-Cooked Beef

Serves 2

3 mushrooms

1 slices ginger

½ cup light soy sauce

2 tablespoons dark soy sauce

2 tablespoons Chinese rice wine or dry sherry

2 teaspoons sugar

2 tablespoons plus 2 teaspoons brown sugar

¼ teaspoon five-spice powder

1 tablespoon oil for stir-frying

1 garlic clove, minced

½ pound boneless stewing beef, cut into chunks

2 cups water

Don't have any stewing beef? Red cooking is a nice way to add flavor to less popular cuts of meat, such as liver.

1. Soak the dried mushrooms in hot water for at least 20 minutes to soften. Gently squeeze to remove any excess water, and slice. Peel the ginger, if desired.
2. Combine the light soy sauce, dark soy sauce, rice wine, white sugar, brown sugar, and five-spice powder; set aside.
3. Add oil to a preheated wok or skillet. When oil is hot, add the ginger and garlic and stir-fry briefly until aromatic. Add the beef and cook until browned.
4. Add the sauce and 2 cups water. Bring to a boil, then turn down the heat and simmer. After 1 hour, add the dried mushrooms. Simmer for 30 minutes, or until the liquid is reduced.

Make Your Own Sauce for Red Cooking

In red cooking, previously browned meat is stewed in a combination of soy sauce and other ingredients. To make your own red cooking sauce, experiment with different combinations of light and dark soy sauce, rice wine, and other liquid ingredients until you find one you like. For extra flavor, add stronger seasonings such as star anise and dried tangerine peel.

Peppery Beef

 Serves 2–4

1 tablespoon soy sauce

½ teaspoon Chinese rice wine or dry sherry

1¼ teaspoons sugar, divided

¼ teaspoon baking soda

½ pound flank steak, shredded

½ green bell pepper

½ red bell pepper

½ cup chicken stock

2 tablespoons dark soy sauce

3 tablespoons oil for stir-frying

1 clove garlic, minced

1 teaspoon minced ginger

¼ teaspoon chili paste

¼ teaspoon sesame oil

⅛ teaspoon Szechwan peppercorns, roasted and ground

For a less biting dish, forego the chili paste and substitute black pepper for the Szechwan peppercorn.

1. Add the soy sauce, rice wine, ¼ teaspoon sugar, and baking soda to the beef. Marinate the beef for 30 minutes.
2. Remove the seeds from the peppers and cut into thin slices. Combine the chicken stock, dark soy sauce, and 1 teaspoon sugar and set aside.
3. Add 2 tablespoons oil to a preheated wok or skillet. When oil is hot, add the beef and stir-fry until it changes color and is nearly cooked through. Remove from the wok and drain on paper towels.
4. Add 1 tablespoon oil if necessary. Add the garlic, ginger, and chili paste. Stir-fry briefly until aromatic. Add the green peppers, stir-fry briefly, and add the red peppers. Stir-fry the peppers until they have a bright color and are tender.
5. Add the sauce to the middle of the wok and bring to a boil. Stir in the sesame oil. Add the beef. Sprinkle the Szechwan peppercorns over. Mix everything through and serve hot.

The $5 Takeout Cookbook

Beef with Broccoli

 Serves 1–2

½ pound beef steak, such as inside round

1½ teaspoons Chinese rice wine or dry sherry

¾ teaspoon cornstarch

¼ teaspoon baking soda

Brown Sauce (see recipe to follow)

3–4 broccoli stalks with flowerets

⅛ red onion

¾ cup oil for frying

1 garlic clove, minced

Serve this restaurant favorite on a bed of white rice or cooked noodles, accompanied by a few fortune cookies.

1. Cut the beef across the grain into thin strips about 2 inches long. Add the rice wine, cornstarch, and baking soda. Marinate the beef for 1 hour.
2. Blanch the broccoli by plunging into boiling water for about 3 minutes. Drain thoroughly. Separate the flowers and the stalks, and cut the stalks into spears along the diagonal. Chop the red onion.
3. Add ¾ cup oil to a preheated wok or skillet. When oil is hot, velvet the beef by adding it to the hot oil just until it changes color, and quickly removing from the wok. Drain the velveted beef on paper towels.
4. Remove all but 2 tablespoons oil from the wok. Add the garlic and stir-fry briefly until aromatic. Add the broccoli. Stir-fry for a minute and then add the red onion. Stir-fry the broccoli until it turns bright green and the red onion until it is soft and translucent.
5. Give the Brown Sauce a quick stir. Push the vegetables up to the sides and add the sauce into the middle of the wok. Turn up the heat and bring the sauce to a boil, stirring vigorously to thicken. Add the beef back into the wok. Mix everything through and serve hot.

BROWN SAUCE

 Yields about ⅓ cup

½ tablespoon plus 1 teaspoon
  oyster sauce
1½ teaspoons hoisin sauce
½ teaspoon sherry
½ teaspoon soy sauce

¼ teaspoon sugar
¼ cup beef broth or juices
  from cooked meat
1 tablespoon water
½ tablespoon cornstarch

Out of cornstarch? You can substitute flour as a thickener in this recipe—just double the amount to 2 tablespoons.

1. Combine all the ingredients, adding the cornstarch last. Bring to a boil.
2. Cook on medium to medium-low heat, stirring constantly to thicken mixture. The sauce should be neither too thin nor too runny, but thick enough to use as a dip, if desired.

Beef Chow Fun

 Serves 2

2 ounces wide rice noodles

½ cup mung bean sprouts

¼ cup chicken stock or broth

½ teaspoon soy sauce

1 tablespoon oil for stir-frying

½ cup cooked beef, shredded

⅛ teaspoon chili paste

Barbecued pork also works well in this dish. For an interesting juxtaposition of color and texture, serve with Braised Baby Bok Choy (Chapter 15).

1. Soak the rice noodles in hot water for at least 15 minutes to soften. Drain well. Blanch the mung bean sprouts by plunging briefly into boiling water. Drain well.
2. Combine the chicken broth and soy sauce. Set aside.
3. Add oil to a preheated wok or skillet. When oil is hot, add the noodles. Stir-fry briefly, then add the sauce. Mix with the noodles and add the shredded beef. Stir in the chili paste. Add the mung bean sprouts. Mix through and serve hot.

Beef Fried Rice

 Serves 2–3

1 large egg

1¼ tablespoon oyster sauce

¹⁄₁₆ teaspoon salt

¹⁄₁₆ teaspoon pepper

¼ red bell pepper

½ green onion

3–4 tablespoons oil for stir-frying

1 garlic clove, minced

¼ onion, chopped

2 mushrooms, sliced

2 cups cold cooked rice

½ pound cooked beef, cut as desired

½ tablespoon mushroom soy sauce

¼ teaspoon sugar

Concerned about cholesterol? Serve the fried rice without the strips of cooked egg on top.

1. Lightly beat the egg. Stir in the oyster sauce and salt and pepper to taste.
2. Remove the seeds from the red pepper and cut into bite-sized cubes. Cut the green onion into 1-inch slices on the diagonal.
3. Add 2 tablespoons oil to a preheated wok or skillet. When oil is hot, pour the egg mixture into the pan. Cook on medium to medium-high heat, using 2 spatulas to turn it over once. Don't scramble. Remove and cut into thin strips. Set aside.
4. Clean out wok, if necessary. Add 1–2 tablespoons oil. When oil is hot, add the garlic cloves and stir-fry until aromatic. Add the onion. Stir-fry for 1 minute, then add the mushrooms, and then the red pepper. Stir-fry the vegetables until they are tender. Remove.
5. Add 1 tablespoon oil to the wok. When oil is hot, add the rice, stirring to separate the grains. Stir-fry on medium heat for 2–3 minutes, then blend in the vegetables and beef. Stir in the mushroom soy sauce and sugar. Stir in the green onion. Serve hot, topped with the egg strips.

Flavorful Fried Rice

Instead of serving fried rice immediately, try storing it in the refrigerator in a sealed container to use another day. This gives the flavors more time to blend. Just be sure to allow the fried rice to cool completely before storing.

CHAPTER 14

PORK AND POULTRY

Braised Spareribs in Black Bean Sauce

 Serves 2–4

1–1½ pounds spareribs

1 tablespoon fermented black beans

1 garlic clove, minced

2 green onions

3 tablespoons hoisin sauce

3 tablespoons soy sauce

1½ teaspoons sugar

½ cup water

2 tablespoons oil for stir-frying

Savory fermented black beans nicely complement the delicate sweet flavor of pork in this recipe.

1. Wash the spareribs, pat dry, and separate. Mash the black beans with the back edge of a knife or cleaver. Mix with the garlic and a bit of water. Cut the green onions into 1-inch pieces.
2. Combine the hoisin sauce, soy sauce, sugar, and water.
3. Add oil to a preheated wok or skillet. Stir-fry the pork for 2–3 minutes. Add the fermented bean and garlic mixture and stir-fry until aromatic.
4. Add the sauce and bring to a boil. Turn down the heat, cover, and simmer for 20–25 minutes, until the spareribs are cooked. Stir in the green onions or serve as a garnish.

Fermented Black Beans

These are not the dried black beans that enliven many Mexican dishes. Instead, fermented black beans (also called salted black beans) are made with black soybeans that have been fermented in salt, garlic, and a number of spices. Fermented black beans are sold in cans and plastic bags in Asian markets. In a pinch, black bean sauce can be used as a substitute, but the dish won't have the same flavor.

The $5 Takeout Cookbook

Sweet-and-Sour Spareribs

 Serves 3

$ Total Cost: $3.88

1½ pounds spareribs

4 teaspoons sugar, divided

2 tablespoons plus 1 teaspoon rice vinegar, divided

2 tablespoons ketchup

2 tablespoons Worcestershire sauce

4 tablespoons soy sauce

2 tablespoons oil for stir-frying

1. Wash spareribs and pat dry. Separate into serving size pieces. Marinate the ribs in 1 teaspoon sugar and 1 teaspoon rice vinegar for 30 minutes.
2. Mix together 3 teaspoons sugar, 2 tablespoons rice vinegar, ketchup, Worcestershire sauce, and soy sauce, and set aside.
3. Add oil to a preheated wok or skillet. When oil is hot, add the ribs and stir-fry for about 5 minutes, until they brown.
4. Add the sauce, turn down the heat, cover, and simmer the ribs for 45 minutes to 1 hour.

Pork with Young Bamboo Shoots

Serves 2–4

½ pound pork tenderloin

3 teaspoons Chinese rice wine or dry sherry, divided

½ teaspoon sugar

1½ teaspoons cornstarch

8 ounces canned or fresh peeled young bamboo shoots

½ cup chicken stock or broth

1 teaspoon rice vinegar

3 tablespoons oil for stir-frying

Due to their strong flavor, young bamboo shoots are considered to be a great delicacy in China.

1. Cut the pork into thin slices. Add 2 teaspoons of the rice wine, the sugar, and the cornstarch. Marinate the pork for 30 minutes.
2. Blanch the bamboo shoots in boiling water for at least 5 minutes. Drain thoroughly and chop.
3. Combine the chicken stock, 1 teaspoon rice wine, and the rice vinegar, and set aside.
4. Add 2 tablespoons oil to a preheated wok or skillet. When oil is hot, add the pork and stir-fry until it changes color and is nearly cooked. Remove and drain on paper towels.
5. Add 1 tablespoon oil to the wok. Add the bamboo shoots and stir-fry. Add the sauce in the middle of the wok and bring to a boil. Add the pork. Turn down the heat and simmer for 5 minutes. Serve hot.

Why Waste a Wok?
Don't hide your wok in the cupboard when you're not cooking Chinese food. A wok's unusual shape makes it useful for everything from mixing batter to tossing a salad. And nothing beats a wok for turning out scrambled eggs and omelets that don't stick to the bottom of the pan.

Basic Sweet-and-Sour Pork

Serves 2–4

⅔ pound pork loin, center cut, bone in

1 tablespoon soy sauce

1 tablespoon cornstarch

1 teaspoon baking soda

⅔ cup canned pineapple chunks

½ cup reserved pineapple juice

½ red bell pepper

½ green bell pepper

¼ pound baby carrots

⅓ cup rice vinegar

½ cup brown sugar

1 tablespoon Worcestershire sauce

¼ cup ketchup

¼ cup water

3 tablespoons oil for stir-frying

2 teaspoons cornstarch mixed with 4 teaspoons water

For extra flavor, use 2 tablespoons black rice vinegar and ¼ cup white rice vinegar when making the sauce.

1. Cut away the bone from the pork and remove any fat. Cut the pork into cubes. Add the soy sauce, cornstarch, and baking soda to the pork. Marinate the pork in the refrigerator for 1½ hours.
2. Open a can of pineapple chunks and remove ⅔ cup pineapple and ½ cup juice. Blanch the peppers and carrots by plunging briefly into boiling water. Remove the seeds from the green and red peppers, and cut into cubes. Cut the carrots in half.
3. Bring the rice vinegar, brown sugar, Worcestershire sauce, ketchup, reserved pineapple juice, and water to a boil. Turn down the heat to low and keep warm.
4. Add 2 tablespoons oil to a preheated wok or skillet. When oil is hot, add the pork. Stir-fry until it changes color and is nearly cooked through. Remove from the wok and drain on paper towels.
5. Add 1 tablespoon oil. When oil is hot, add the carrots. Stir-fry for a minute and add the red and green peppers.
6. Bring the sauce back up to a boil. Add the cornstarch-and-water mixture, stirring vigorously to thicken. Mix the pineapple in with the sauce. Push the vegetables up to the sides of the wok and add the sauce in the middle. Add the pork back into the wok. Mix through and serve hot.

Traditional Mu Shu Pork

Serves 2

¼ pound boneless pork chops

1½ green onions, divided

½ tablespoon soy sauce

¼ teaspoon sesame oil

1 teaspoon cornstarch

¼ teaspoon baking soda

¾ cup fresh mushrooms

5 fresh water chestnuts

¼ cup reserved mushroom liquid

1 tablespoon dark soy sauce

1 teaspoon sugar

⅛ teaspoon sesame oil

1 egg

⅛ teaspoon salt

1½–2½ tablespoons oil for stir-frying

¼ slice ginger

¼ cup canned bamboo shoots, rinsed

½ recipe Mandarin Pancakes (see recipe to follow)

⅛ cup hoisin sauce

1. Trim any fat from the pork and cut into thin strips. Add 1 chopped green onion, soy sauce, sesame oil, cornstarch, and baking soda. Marinate the pork for 30 minutes.
2. Soak the dried mushrooms, dried lily buds, and wood fungus in hot water for at least 20 minutes to soften. Reserve the mushroom soaking liquid. Give the mushrooms a gentle squeeze to remove any excess water and thinly slice. Cut the remaining ½ green onion into 1-inch pieces. Peel the fresh water chestnuts and cut in half.
3. Combine the reserved mushroom liquid, dark soy sauce, sugar, and sesame oil and set aside.
4. Lightly beat the eggs and stir in ⅛ teaspoon salt. Add 1 tablespoon oil to a preheated wok or skillet. When oil is hot, scramble the egg. Remove from the wok and set aside.
5. Add 1 more tablespoon oil. When oil is hot, add the pork strips and stir-fry until they turn white and are nearly cooked through. Add the ginger and green onions and stir-fry briefly. Add the mushrooms, lily buds, wood fungus, bamboo shoots, and water chestnuts. Add the sauce and bring to a boil. Add the pork and the scrambled egg. Mix everything through.
6. To serve, brush a pancake with the hoisin sauce, add a generous helping of Mu Shu Pork, and roll up the pancake.

MANDARIN PANCAKES

 Yields 4–5 Pancakes

$ Total Cost: $1.49

1 cup all-purpose flour
½ cup boiling water
⅛ cup sesame oil

Add water slowly until you are sure how much is needed. Everything from altitude to the age of the flour can affect the amount required.

1. Place the flour in a large bowl. Add the boiling water and quickly stir with a wooden spoon.
2. As soon as you can withstand the heat, knead the warm dough on a lightly floured surface until it is smooth. Cover with a damp cloth and let stand for 30 minutes.
3. Cut the dough in half. Roll each half into a 9-inch cylinder. Using a tape measure, lightly score and cut the dough into 1-inch pieces. You will have 18 pieces at this point.
4. Shape each piece into a ball and then flatten into a circle between the palms of your hands. Brush the top of each piece with sesame oil, and then place the pieces on top of each other, oiled sides together.
5. Using a lightly floured rolling pin, roll the pieces into a 5½–6-inch circle. (Don't worry if the edges overlap.) Continue with the rest of the dough.
6. Heat a dry pan on low-medium heat. When the pan is hot, add one of the paired pancakes and cook on each side for 2 minutes or until brown bubbles appear (the second side will cook more quickly). Remove from the pan and pull the pancakes apart while they are still hot. Place on a plate and cover with a damp cloth while cooking the remainder.

Pancakes for Dinner

Besides making a tasty snack, mandarin pancakes are served with the northern dishes mu shu pork and Peking duck. In the case of mu shu pork, the pork is wrapped in the pancakes, which are brushed with hoisin sauce.

Pork Chop Suey

 Serves 2

¼ pound pork tenderloin

1 teaspoon Chinese rice wine or dry sherry

1 teaspoon soy sauce

1 teaspoon baking soda

1 green onions, thinly sliced on the diagonal

1 tablespoon oyster sauce

1 tablespoon chicken broth or stock

½ teaspoon sugar

2–3 tablespoons oil for stir-frying

3 fresh mushrooms, thinly sliced

½ stalk celery, thinly sliced on the diagonal

1 stalks bok choy including leaves, thinly sliced on the diagonal

1 4-ounce can bamboo shoots, drained

Vegetables take center stage in this dish; the meat is there only to add a bit of flavor.

1. Cut the pork into thin slices. Marinate the pork with the rice wine, soy sauce, and baking soda for 30 minutes.
2. Combine the oyster sauce, chicken broth, and sugar. Set aside.
3. Add 2 tablespoons oil to a preheated wok or skillet. When oil is hot, add the pork. Stir-fry until it changes color and is nearly cooked through. Remove from the wok.
4. Add 1–2 tablespoons oil. When oil is hot, add the mushrooms and stir-fry for about 1 minute. Add the celery and the bok choy stalks, then the bamboo shoots, stir-frying each for about 1 minute in the middle of the wok before adding the next vegetable. (If the wok is too crowded, stir-fry each vegetable separately.) Add more oil as necessary, pushing the vegetables up to the side of the wok until the oil is heated. Add the bok choy leaves and the green onion.
5. Add the sauce to the middle of the wok and bring to a boil. Add the pork. Mix everything through and serve hot.

The $5 Takeout Cookbook

Spicy Hoisin Pork

 Serves 2

½ pound pork tenderloin

½ tablespoon soy sauce

1 teaspoon baking soda

½ bunch spinach

1 tablespoon hoisin sauce

½ tablespoon dark soy sauce

⅛ cup water

1½ tablespoon oil for stir-frying

⅛ teaspoon chili paste

For a less spicy dish, substitute ¼ teaspoon chili sauce with garlic for the chili paste.

1. Cut the pork into thin slices. Marinate in the soy sauce and baking soda for 30 minutes.
2. Blanch the spinach briefly in boiling water and drain thoroughly.
3. Combine the hoisin sauce, dark soy sauce, and water. Set aside.
4. Add 1 tablespoon oil to a preheated wok or skillet. When oil is hot, add the pork and stir-fry until it changes color and is nearly cooked through. Remove and drain on paper towels.
5. Add ½ tablespoon oil. When oil is hot, add the chili paste and stir-fry until aromatic. Add the spinach. Stir-fry for a minute, adding sugar or soy sauce to season if desired. Add the sauce in the middle of the wok and bring to a boil. Add the pork. Turn down the heat, mix everything through, and serve hot.

How to Season a Carbon Steel Wok

It's important to properly season a wok before using it for the first time. First, wash the wok in soapy water. Dry thoroughly, then lightly coat the inside surface with vegetable oil, using a paper towel and tilting the wok to ensure even coverage. Heat the wok on low-medium heat for 10 minutes. Remove to a cool burner and wipe off the inside with a paper towel. Repeat this process several times. The wok is ready to use when the paper towel doesn't pick up any black residue.

Pork in Bean Sauce

Serves 2

$ Total Cost: $2.67

½ pound pork tenderloin chops, boneless

½ tablespoon oyster sauce

¼ teaspoon sugar

¾ teaspoon cornstarch

1 tablespoon black bean sauce

1 tablespoon dark soy sauce

1 teaspoon Chinese rice wine or dry sherry

1 teaspoon sugar

⅛ teaspoon salt

⅛ cup water

⅛ teaspoon sesame oil

1 tablespoon oil for stir-frying

⅛ teaspoon chili paste

Szechwan and Cantonese Cooking

Fiery Szechwan cuisine is famous for its "mouthburners"—dishes such as Kung Pao Chicken and Mapo Tofu made with hot chilies and Szechwan peppercorns. Reputed to represent the best of Chinese cooking, Cantonese cuisine features fresh ingredients that are subtly seasoned and not overcooked. Cantonese cooks pride themselves on allowing the natural flavors of the ingredients to come through in dishes such as Sweet-and-Sour Pork and Lobster Cantonese.

1. Cut the pork into thin strips. Add the oyster sauce, sugar, and cornstarch, adding the cornstarch last. Marinate the pork for 30 minutes.
2. Combine the black bean sauce, dark soy sauce, rice wine, sugar, salt, water, and sesame oil, and set aside.
3. Add oil to a preheated wok or skillet. When oil is hot, add the chili paste and stir-fry briefly until aromatic. Add the pork. Stir-fry until it changes color and is nearly cooked through.
4. Push the pork up to the side of the wok and add the sauce in the middle. Bring to a boil. Mix the sauce with the pork. Cover and simmer for a few minutes until the pork is cooked through.

The $5 Takeout Cookbook

Five-Spice Spareribs

 Serves 3

Total Cost: $3.89

1½ pounds spareribs

2 garlic cloves, smashed and peeled

3 tablespoons soy sauce

1 teaspoon sesame oil

1 tablespoon Chinese rice wine or dry sherry

2 teaspoons brown sugar

1 teaspoon hot chili oil

½ teaspoon Szechwan Salt and Pepper Mix (see recipe to follow)

½ teaspoon five-spice powder, or to taste

2 tablespoons water

These spicy ribs nicely complement a less highly seasoned dish such as Three Vegetable Stir-Fry (Chapter 15).

1. Mix together all the ingredients except for the spareribs. Marinate the spareribs for 30 minutes. Reserve the marinade.
2. Preheat oven to 350°F. Brush half of the reserved marinade on the spareribs and roast for 15 minutes. Brush on the rest of marinade and roast the spareribs for another 15 minutes or until they are cooked.

SZECHWAN SALT AND PEPPER MIX

 Yields about ⅓ cup

Total Cost: $1.28

2 tablespoons Szechwan peppercorns

1 teaspoon black peppercorns

½ teaspoon white peppercorns

¼ cup salt

1. Brown the peppercorns and salt in a heavy skillet on medium to medium-low heat, shaking the pan occasionally, until the Szechwan peppercorns are fragrant and the salt turns a light brown color.
2. Grind the cooled mixture in a blender. Store in a sealed jar and use as a dip or condiment.

Twice Cooked Pork

 Serves 2–4

 Total Cost: $4.42

½ pound boneless pork
½ red bell pepper
½ green bell pepper
1 clove garlic, chopped
2 slices ginger, chopped

3 tablespoons oil for stir-frying
1 teaspoon hot bean paste
2 tablespoons dark soy sauce
1 teaspoon sugar

Pork is cooked twice in this simple but popular Szechwan dish. Serve on a bed of steamed rice or noodles.

1. Boil the pork in water for 20–25 minutes. Remove and cool. Cut into thin strips.
2. Blanch the peppers by plunging briefly into boiling water. Cut into thin slices.
3. Add 3 tablespoons oil to a preheated wok or skillet. When oil is hot, add the ginger, garlic, and hot bean paste with garlic. Stir-fry briefly until the garlic and ginger are aromatic. Add the peppers and stir-fry. Mix in the dark soy sauce and sugar. Add the pork. Combine all the ingredients thoroughly and stir-fry for about 1 more minute. Serve hot.

Pork—Not the "Other White Meat"

Pork may be the "other white meat" in the West, but in China the words *pork* and *meat* are virtually synonymous. When it comes to beef, cows and oxen have traditionally been valued more as work animals than as the main source of protein at the dinner table. By contrast, economical pigs are cheaper to feed, requiring less grazing space. While beef is now widely enjoyed in northern China, it is still not uncommon for southern Chinese families to rely primarily on pork as their main source of meat.

The $5 Takeout Cookbook

Egg Foo Yung with Pork

 Serves 3

⅛ red bell pepper

⅓ cup mung bean sprouts

½ stalk celery

½ cup cooked pork, cut into small pieces

2–3 tablespoons oil for stir-frying

¼ teaspoon salt, divided

3 eggs

¹⁄₁₆ teaspoon pepper

½ teaspoon Chinese rice wine or dry sherry

2 button mushroom caps, thinly sliced

Barbecued or roast pork works well in this recipe. Be sure to remove any bones before adding the pork to the egg mixture.

1. Remove the seeds from the red pepper and cut into thin slices about 1 inch long. Blanch the bean sprouts by plunging briefly into boiling water. Blanch the celery by plunging into the boiling water and boiling for 2–3 minutes. Drain the blanched vegetables thoroughly. Cut the celery into thin slices on the diagonal.
2. Add 2 teaspoons oil to a preheated wok or skillet. When the oil is hot, add the celery and stir-fry on medium high heat. Add ⅛ teaspoon salt. Remove the cooked celery from the wok.
3. Lightly beat the eggs. Stir in the pepper, ⅛ teaspoon salt, and the rice wine. Add the pork and vegetables, mixing well.
4. Add 2 tablespoons oil to a preheated wok or skillet. When the oil is hot, add one-sixth of the egg mixture. Cook until the bottom is cooked, then turn over and cook the other side. Continue with the remainder of the egg mixture, making 3 omelets. Add more oil while cooking as necessary. Serve with an egg foo yung sauce or soy sauce.

Egg Rolls

 Yields 15 egg rolls

¼ cup canned bamboo shoots, sliced

1 tablespoon oyster sauce

1 tablespoon chicken broth or stock

½ teaspoon sugar

2 tablespoons oil for stir-frying

6 large fresh mushrooms, thinly sliced

1 stalk celery, thinly sliced on the diagonal

¼ cup water chestnuts, thinly sliced

1 cup fresh mung bean sprouts, drained

2 green onions, thinly sliced on the diagonal

½ pound barbecued pork

15 egg roll wrappers

3 tablespoons cornstarch mixed with 2 tablespoons water

4–6 cups oil for frying

This wrapping method allows you to add more filling than the traditional "envelope" method. Firmly sealing the edges prevents oil from entering during deep-frying.

1. Thinly slice the bamboo shoots. Combine the oyster sauce, chicken broth, and sugar. Set aside.
2. Add 2 tablespoons oil to a preheated wok or skillet. When oil is hot, add the mushrooms and stir-fry for about 1 minute. Add the celery, then the water chestnuts, then bamboo shoots, stir-frying each for about 1 minute in the middle of the wok before adding the next vegetable. (If the wok is too crowded, stir-fry each vegetable separately.) Add more oil as necessary, pushing the vegetables up to the side of the wok until the oil is hot. Add the bean sprouts and the green onions.
3. Add the sauce to the middle of the wok and bring to a boil. Add the barbecued pork. Heat everything through. Cool.
4. Heat 4–6 cups oil to 375°F. While the oil is heating, prepare the egg roll wrappers. To wrap, spread a heaping tablespoon of filling in the middle of the wrapper, evenly spread out but not too close to the edges. Coat the top edge and the sides with the cornstarch/water mixture. Fold the bottom half over the filling. Fold the top half over, making sure the 2 sides overlap. Press down to seal all the edges. Continue with the remainder of the egg rolls. (Prepare more cornstarch and water if necessary.)
5. Deep-fry the egg rolls until they turn golden brown (2–3 minutes). Drain on paper towels.

Yangchow Fried Rice

 Serves 2

1 large egg

1 tablespoon oyster sauce, divided

Salt and pepper, to taste

2 cups cold cooked rice

½ green onion

3 tablespoons oil for stir-frying

⅛ pound (4 ounces) fresh shrimp, peeled and deveined

¼ cup baby carrots, halved

¼ cup peas

¼ teaspoon sugar

½ cup barbecued pork, cubed

This colorful dish flecked with yellow, orange, green, and pink is named for the city of Yangchow in Jiangsu province, famous for its rice dishes.

1. Lightly beat the egg. Stir in 1 tablespoon oyster sauce, and a small amount of salt and pepper to taste. Mix the egg in with the rice, stirring to separate the grains.
2. Cut the green onion into 1-inch pieces on the diagonal.
3. Add 1 tablespoon oil to a preheated wok or heavy skillet. When oil is hot, add the shrimp. Stir-fry briefly until it turns pink. Remove and drain on paper towels.
4. Clean out wok and add 1 tablespoon oil. When oil is hot, add the baby carrots. Stir-fry for 1 minute, then add the green peas. Stir-fry until the peas are bright green. Remove.
5. Wipe the wok clean and add 1 tablespoon oil. When oil is hot, add the rice and egg mixture. Stir-fry for 2–3 minutes, then add 1 tablespoon oyster sauce and the sugar. Add the barbecued pork and shrimp. Add the vegetables. Stir in the green onion and serve hot.

Pork Chow Mein

 Serves 3

½ pound fresh noodles

⅛ teaspoon sesame oil

½ pound pork tenderloin

½ tablespoon Chinese rice wine or dry sherry

⅛ teaspoon salt

1¼ cup shredded napa cabbage

2 large dried mushrooms

¼ green or red bell pepper

⅙ cup chicken broth

⅛ cup water

1/16 cup reserved mushroom soaking liquid

½ tablespoon plus 1 teaspoon oyster sauce

1/16 teaspoon salt

2–3 tablespoons oil for stir-frying

1 garlic clove, minced

½ carrot, diced

½ stalk celery, thinly sliced on the diagonal

½ cup mung bean sprouts, rinsed and drained

½ teaspoon cornstarch mixed with 4 teaspoons water

½ teaspoon sugar

The mushroom soaking liquid adds an earthy flavor to this dish. You can also use fresh mushrooms and ¼ cup water instead.

1. Boil the noodles according to the instructions on the package, using chopsticks to separate. Drain and toss with sesame oil.
2. Cut pork into cubes and marinate with rice wine and ⅛ teaspoon salt for 30 minutes.
3. Soak the dried mushrooms for at least 20 minutes to soften. Reserve soaking liquid. Thinly slice mushrooms. Remove the seeds from the pepper and cut into cubes.
4. Combine chicken broth, water, mushroom soaking liquid, oyster sauce. Set aside.

The $5 Takeout Cookbook

Pork Chow Mein—*cont'd*

5. Add 2 tablespoons oil to a preheated wok or skillet. Add the pork and stir-fry until it changes color and is nearly cooked. Remove and drain on paper towels.

6. Add ½ tablespoon oil. When oil is hot, add the noodles and stir-fry until they turn light brown. Remove and keep warm. Clean out the wok with a paper towel.

7. Add ½ tablespoon oil. When oil is hot, add the garlic and stir-fry briefly until aromatic. Either stir-fry the carrot, celery, pepper, dried mushrooms, cabbage, and bean sprouts together or separately, adding one at a time and adding more oil as needed. (Move the vegetables up to the side of the wok and wait until oil is heated.)

8. Add the sauce to the middle of the wok and bring to a boil. Add the cornstarch-and-water mixture, stirring quickly to thicken. Add the sugar. Add the pork and heat through. Serve hot over the noodles.

Mad about Mein!

Mein is the Chinese word for noodles. When it comes to important staple foods, noodles rank second only to rice in the Chinese diet. Noodles are steamed, stir-fried, added to soups, and used to make dumplings. Although noodles are enjoyed throughout China, they are particularly important in the north, where a harsher climate prohibits the cultivation of rice crops.

Basic Chicken Stir-Fry

 Serves 2–3

½ pound chicken meat

1 tablespoon oil for stir-frying

½ garlic clove, minced

1 thin slices ginger

¼ cup chicken stock or broth

½ tablespoon Chinese rice wine or dry sherry

½ teaspoon sugar

⅛ teaspoon salt

The Base of Many Chicken Recipes

Basic Chicken Stir-Fry is a skeleton recipe that you can adapt according to your tastes and the ingredients you have on hand. Add a marinade and experiment with different seasonings such as chili paste. To make a one-dish meal that includes vegetables, stir-fry the chicken first and remove it from the wok. Stir-fry the vegetables and add the sauce. Add the chicken back and simmer until the meat is cooked. For longer-cooking pieces of meat such as chicken legs, increase the amount of broth and simmer the chicken for 20–30 minutes or until the meat is cooked through.

Simmering the chicken in broth and seasonings brings out its natural flavors. Serve with Stir-Fried Bok Choy (Chapter 15) for a quick and easy meal.

1. Wash the chicken meat, pat dry, and cut into cubes or thin slices.
2. Add oil to a preheated wok or skillet. When oil is hot, add the garlic and ginger. Stir-fry briefly until aromatic. Add the chicken and stir-fry until it changes color.
3. Add the chicken stock, rice wine, sugar, and salt and bring to a boil. Simmer, covered, until the chicken is cooked.

Moo Goo Gai Pan

 Serves 2

1 large boneless, skinless chicken breasts

2 tablespoons oyster sauce, divided

1 teaspoon cornstarch, divided

¼ cup chicken stock or broth

½ teaspoon sugar

$\frac{1}{16}$ teaspoon white pepper

¼ cup fresh mushrooms

2 tablespoons oil for stir-frying

½ clove garlic, minced

½ 4-ounce can bamboo shoots, rinsed

The marriage of chicken and mushrooms is central to this dish, but feel free to substitute other vegetables for the bamboo shoots.

1. Wash the chicken and cut into thin slices. Mix in 2 tablespoons oyster sauce and 1 teaspoon cornstarch. Marinate the chicken for 30 minutes.
2. Mix together the chicken stock, sugar, white pepper, 2 tablespoons oyster sauce, and 1 teaspoon cornstarch. Set aside. Wipe the mushrooms clean with a damp cloth and thinly slice.
3. Add 1 tablespoon oil to a preheated wok or skillet. When oil is hot, add the garlic and stir-fry briefly until aromatic. Add the chicken and stir-fry until it changes color and is nearly cooked through. Remove the chicken from the wok and set aside.
4. Wipe the wok clean and add 1 more tablespoon oil. When the oil is hot, add the mushrooms and stir-fry for about 1 minute. Add the bamboo shoots.
5. Give the sauce a quick stir. Make a well in the middle of the wok by pushing the vegetables up to the sides. Add the sauce in the middle, stirring vigorously to thicken. Add the chicken and mix through.

Lemony Chicken Stir-Fry

 Serves 2–4

2 large skinless, boneless chicken breasts

2 tablespoons Chinese rice wine or dry sherry, divided

3 teaspoons soy sauce, divided

3 tablespoons plus ½ teaspoon freshly squeezed lemon juice, divided

1 teaspoon cornstarch

½ cup water

2 tablespoons brown sugar

1 teaspoon honey

3–4 tablespoons oil for stir-frying

1 clove garlic, minced

1 teaspoon minced ginger

1 teaspoon cornstarch mixed with 4 teaspoons water

Sweet brown sugar nicely balances tart lemon juice in this recipe.

1. Cut the chicken into thin strips. Add 1 tablespoon rice wine, 1 teaspoon soy sauce, ½ teaspoon lemon juice, and 1 teaspoon cornstarch to the chicken, adding the cornstarch last. Marinate the chicken for 30 minutes.
2. Mix together 3 tablespoons freshly squeezed lemon juice, water, 1 tablespoon rice wine, 2 teaspoons soy sauce, brown sugar, and honey. Set aside.
3. Add 2 tablespoons oil to a preheated wok or skillet. When oil is hot, add the chicken and stir-fry until it changes color and is nearly cooked. Remove from the wok and set aside.
4. Clean out the wok with a paper towel. Preheat and add 1½ tablespoons oil. When oil is hot, add the garlic and ginger. Stir-fry briefly until aromatic. Add the sauce, bringing to a boil.
5. Give the cornstarch-and-water mixture a quick stir. Add to the sauce, stirring vigorously to thicken. Add the chicken and heat through.

Why Marinate?

Although it can seem time consuming, never forego marinating meat if a recipe calls for it. Besides lending flavor, a good marinade tenderizes the meat as well. It's rare to find a Chinese recipe that doesn't call for marinating meat prior to stir-frying.

The $5 Takeout Cookbook

Steamed Lemon Chicken

 Serves 1–2

1 chicken breast

1 tablespoon minced ginger

1½ tablespoons freshly squeezed lemon juice

¼ cup water

2 teaspoons Chinese rice wine or dry sherry

1 teaspoon soy sauce

1½ teaspoons sugar

½ teaspoon black rice vinegar

1 teaspoon cornstarch

This recipe provides a generous helping of sauce to mix with rice and other vegetables.

1. Place the chicken in a heatproof plate on a bamboo steamer. Add the minced ginger. Steam for 20 minutes, or until the chicken turns white and is cooked.
2. While the chicken is steaming, mix together the lemon juice, water, rice wine, soy sauce, sugar, black rice vinegar, and cornstarch. In a small saucepan, heat the sauce to boiling. Pour over the steamed chicken.

General Tso's Chicken

Serves 2

½ pound dark chicken meat

1 tablespoon soy sauce

1½ teaspoons Chinese rice wine or dry sherry, divided

1⁄16 teaspoon white pepper

½ tablespoon cornstarch

2 tablespoons dark soy sauce

1 teaspoon sugar

¼ teaspoon sesame oil

3 dried red chilies

2–3 cups oil for deep-frying

½ large clove garlic, minced

½ teaspoon minced ginger

1 green onions, thinly sliced

To serve a vegetable with this dish, stir-fry while you are waiting for the oil to heat up for deep-frying.

1. Cut the chicken into cubes. Mix in the soy sauce, 1 teaspoon of the rice wine, white pepper, and the cornstarch, adding the cornstarch last. Marinate the chicken for 30 minutes.
2. Combine the dark soy sauce, sugar, sesame oil, and ½ teaspoon rice wine. Set aside. Cut the red chilies in half and remove the seeds. Chop and set aside.
3. Heat the oil to 350°F. When the oil is hot, add the chicken cubes and deep-fry until they are lightly browned. Remove from the wok and drain on paper towels.
4. Raise the temperature of the wok to 400°F. Deep-fry the chicken a second time briefly, until the chicken turns golden brown. Remove from the wok and drain on paper towels.
5. Drain the wok, leaving 2 tablespoons of oil for stir-frying. When the oil is hot, add the garlic, ginger, and green onions. Stir-fry briefly until aromatic. Add the chilies and cook for 1 minute. Add the sauce in the middle of the wok and bring to a boil. Add the chicken and mix through.

Food Fit for a General

General Tso's Chicken is named after a famous military leader who helped quash China's Taipeng rebellion in the mid-1800s. How the dish came to be named after General Tso is lost to history, although he was rumored to have a penchant for fiery foods.

Quick and Easy Orange Chicken

 Serves 2

1 large boneless, skinless chicken breasts, about 7 ounces each

1 tablespoon Chinese rice wine or dry sherry

1 egg white

2 ½ teaspoons cornstarch, divided

⅛ cup water

2 ½ teaspoons freshly squeezed orange juice

½ tablespoon soy sauce

¾ teaspoon brown sugar

⅛ teaspoon chili paste

⅛ teaspoon sesame oil

1 tablespoon oil for stir-frying

½ teaspoon minced ginger

½ clove garlic, minced

Serve with rice and a steamed vegetable for a quick and easy dish on busy weeknights.

1. Cut the chicken into 1-inch cubes. Mix in the rice wine, egg white, and 1½ teaspoons cornstarch, adding the cornstarch last. Marinate the chicken for 15 minutes.
2. Mix together the water, orange juice, soy sauce, brown sugar, chili paste, sesame oil, and 1 teaspoon cornstarch.
3. Add oil to a preheated wok or skillet. When the oil is ready, add the ginger and garlic. Stir-fry briefly until aromatic.
4. Add the chicken and stir-fry until the chicken changes color and is nearly cooked through.
5. Give the sauce a quick stir. Push the chicken up the sides of the wok and add the sauce, stirring vigorously to thicken. Mix the sauce with the chicken and cook the chicken for another minute.

Kung Pao Stir-Fry

 Serves 2–4

2 boneless, skinless chicken breasts

1 tablespoon soy sauce

2 tablespoons Chinese rice wine or dry sherry, divided

1 tablespoon cornstarch

2 tablespoons dark soy sauce

1 teaspoon sugar

¼ teaspoon sesame oil

4 tablespoons oil for stir-frying

1 clove garlic, minced

¼ teaspoon chili paste

½ cup unsalted, roasted peanuts

This healthier version of Kung Pao Chicken uses less oil but still contains protein-rich peanuts.

1. Cut the chicken into 1-inch cubes. Add the soy sauce, 1 tablespoon rice wine, and the cornstarch to the chicken, adding the cornstarch last. Marinate the chicken for 30 minutes.
2. Mix together the dark soy sauce, 1 tablespoon rice wine, sugar, and sesame oil.
3. Add 2 tablespoons oil to a preheated wok or skillet. When oil is hot, add the chicken cubes and stir-fry until they turn golden. Remove the chicken from the wok and drain on paper towels.
4. Add 2 tablespoons oil. When oil is hot, add the garlic clove and chili paste. Stir-fry briefly until aromatic. Add the peanuts and stir-fry very briefly, taking care not to burn.
5. Add the sauce to the wok and bring to a boil. Turn down the heat and add the chicken. Mix everything and simmer for a few minutes until the chicken is cooked through.

The $5 Takeout Cookbook

Sesame Chicken

 Serves 2–3

1½ whole boneless chicken breasts

1 tablespoon soy sauce

½ tablespoon Chinese rice wine or dry sherry

¹⁄₁₆ teaspoon sesame oil

1 tablespoon flour

⅛ teaspoon baking powder

⅛ teaspoon baking soda

1 tablespoon water

3 tablespoons cornstarch, divided

½ teaspoon vegetable oil

¼ cup water

½ cup chicken stock or broth

1 tablespoon dark soy sauce

¼ cup vinegar

1 teaspoon chili sauce with garlic

½ large clove garlic, minced

½ teaspoon rice vinegar

½ cup sugar

1 tablespoon sesame seeds

2–3 cups oil for deep-frying

The secret to this popular restaurant dish lies in the sauce—adjust the sweetness level by increasing or decreasing the ratio of vinegar to sugar.

1. Cut the chicken into cubes. Mix in the soy sauce, rice wine, sesame oil, flour, baking powder, baking soda, water, 1 tablespoon cornstarch, and vegetable oil. Marinate the chicken for 30 minutes.
2. In a medium bowl, combine ¼ cup water, chicken stock, dark soy sauce, vinegar, chili sauce with garlic, garlic clove, rice vinegar, sugar, and 2 tablespoons cornstarch. Set aside.
3. Heat oil in wok to 350°F. Add the marinated chicken and deep-fry until golden brown. Remove from the wok with a slotted spoon and drain on paper towels.
4. Raise the oil temperature in the wok to 400°F. Deep-fry the chicken a second time, until it turns golden brown. Remove and drain.
5. Give the sauce a quick stir. Bring to a boil in a medium-sized saucepan. Pour over the deep-fried chicken. Garnish with the sesame seeds.

Spicy Braised Chicken Wings

 Serves 2–3

6 chicken wings

⅛ cup chicken broth

¼ cup plain yogurt

½ tablespoon Chinese rice
    wine or dry sherry

½ tablespoon soy sauce

½ teaspoon honey

½ tablespoon curry paste

2 cups oil for deep-frying

Madras, a hot curry paste made with turmeric, chili, cumin, and coriander, works well in this recipe.

1. Chop the chicken wings into pieces. In a large saucepan, blanch the chicken wing pieces in boiling water for 2 minutes. Drain.
2. Combine the chicken broth, yogurt, rice wine, soy sauce, honey, and curry paste. Set aside.
3. Heat oil for deep-frying. When the oil reaches 350°F, carefully slide the chicken wing pieces into the wok. Deep-fry until they turn light brown. Remove with a slotted spoon and drain on paper towels.
4. Bring the sauce to a boil in a skillet or wok. Add the chicken pieces, cover, and simmer for 10–15 minutes, or until the chicken is cooked through.

Chicken Glazed in Bean Sauce

Serves 2–4

2 large boneless, skinless chicken breasts (12–14 ounces)

2 tablespoons Chinese rice wine or dry sherry

1 tablespoon soy sauce

2½ green onions, thinly sliced on the diagonal

½ cup chicken stock or broth

1 tablespoon dark soy sauce

1 tablespoon bean sauce

2 tablespoons brown sugar

1 clove garlic, chopped

2 tablespoons oil for stir-frying

1 teaspoon cornstarch mixed with 4 teaspoons water

This recipe produces a tender chicken lightly glazed with savory bean sauce. For added protein, try stirring in cashews or peanuts before serving.

1. Wash the chicken breasts, pat dry, and dice.
2. Mix together the rice wine, soy sauce, and half of a green onion. Marinate the chicken for 1 hour.
3. In a small bowl, combine the chicken stock, dark soy sauce, bean sauce, brown sugar, and garlic. Set aside.
4. Add oil to a preheated wok or skillet. When oil is hot, add the chicken and stir-fry until it is nearly cooked through. Remove from the wok and set aside.
5. Add the sauce into the wok. Add the cornstarch-and-water mixture in the middle, stirring vigorously to thicken. Add the chicken, mixing in and letting the sauce reduce until it is a glaze. Stir in the 2 sliced green onions.

Chicken with Red and Green Peppers

 Serves 2–4

2 boneless, skinless chicken breasts
1 tablespoon soy sauce
1 egg white
1½ teaspoons cornstarch
1 green bell pepper
1 red bell pepper
¼ cup water

1½ teaspoons sugar
1 tablespoon black bean sauce
¼ teaspoon chili paste
1 tablespoon cornstarch
3–4 tablespoons oil for stir-frying
2 garlic cloves, chopped
½ cup chopped red onion

1. Chop the chicken into 1½-inch cubes. Mix in the soy sauce, egg white, and cornstarch, being sure to add the cornstarch last. Marinate the chicken for 30 minutes.
2. Wash the green and red peppers, remove the seeds, and cut into chunks.
3. To make the sauce, mix together the water, sugar, black bean sauce, chili paste, and cornstarch, and set aside.
4. Add 2 tablespoons oil to a preheated wok or skillet. When the oil is hot, add the chopped garlic and stir-fry briefly until aromatic. Add the marinated chicken to the wok. Stir-fry until the chicken turns white and is nearly cooked through. Remove from the wok and set aside.
5. Add 2 tablespoons oil. When oil is hot, add the green pepper and onion. Stir-fry for about 1 minute, and then add the red pepper. Stir-fry until the peppers turn a bright color and the onion is softened.
6. Give the sauce a quick stir. Push the vegetables up to the side of the wok and add the sauce in the middle, stirring vigorously to thicken. Mix with the vegetables. Add the chicken. Mix all the ingredients and serve hot.

Quick Red Bell Peppers
Although they are both members of the capsicum family, red peppers have a shorter cooking time than green peppers. For best results, add them at a later stage in stir-frying.

The $5 Takeout Cookbook

Bang Bang Chicken

Serves 2

½ pound boneless, skinless
chicken breasts

Spicy Szechwan Peanut Sauce
(see recipe to follow)

½ large dried bean curd sheet

1 small cucumbers

¼ teaspoon salt

To use Chinese noodles instead of bean curd sheets,
cook the noodles according to instructions, drain well,
and lay over the cucumber slices.

1. Boil chicken breasts in water for 15–20 minutes. Drain well.
2. Cut the bean curd sheet into 4 squares. Soak the sheet in
   cold water to soften. Peel the cucumbers and slice, toss
   with salt, and leave for 15 minutes.
3. Chop the chicken meat into thin slices. Lay the cucumber
   slices on a plate and top with a bean curd sheet. Top with
   the chicken and the sauce. Serve the remainder of the sauce
   in a dipping bowl so guests can help themselves.

SPICY SZECHWAN PEANUT SAUCE

Yields ¼ cup

1½ tablespoon peanut butter

1½ tablespoon soy sauce

2 teaspoons sugar

1½ tablespoon black rice
vinegar

½ tablespoon sesame oil

½ clove garlic, chopped

½–1 tablespoon hot chili oil

Process all the ingredients in a food processor, and use as a dipping sauce.

Chicken with Walnuts

 Serves 2–3

1 boneless, skinless chicken breasts

1 egg white

⅛ teaspoon salt

1 teaspoon cornstarch

¾ tablespoons dark soy sauce

1½ tablespoon oyster sauce

¾ tablespoons Chinese rice wine or dry sherry

1⅛ teaspoons sugar

¼ cup water

¼ cup walnut halves

½ garlic clove, smashed

½ teaspoon cornstarch mixed with 4 teaspoons water

½ cup oil for frying

The crunchy texture of walnuts goes well with velvety chicken cooked in a savory sauce.

1. Cut the chicken into 1-inch cubes. Mix in the egg white, salt, and cornstarch, adding the cornstarch last. Marinate the chicken for 30 minutes.
2. Combine the dark soy sauce, oyster sauce, rice wine, sugar, and water, and set aside.
3. Boil the walnuts in water for at least 5 minutes. Drain and dry.
4. Add ½ cup oil to a preheated wok or skillet. When oil is hot, add the chicken cubes. Velvet the chicken cubes by submerging them in the hot oil just until they change color. Remove immediately and drain on paper towels.
5. Remove all but 1 tablespoon oil. When oil is hot, add the garlic and stir-fry until aromatic. Add the walnuts and stir-fry for about 1 minute. Push up to the side of the wok and add the sauce in the middle. Bring to a boil.
6. Give the cornstarch-and-water mixture a quick stir. Add in the middle of the wok, stirring quickly to thicken. Add the chicken. Mix everything together. Cover and simmer for a few minutes until the chicken is cooked through.

Chengdu Chicken

Serves 2

2 boneless, skinless chicken breasts

1 stalks celery

1½ teaspoons red or black rice vinegar

½ teaspoon sugar

½ teaspoon salt, divided

¼ cup hot water

½ teaspoon Chinese rice wine or dry sherry

1½ tablespoon oil for stir-frying

½ tablespoon chopped ginger

1 garlic clove, chopped

1 tablespoon hot bean sauce

1 teaspoon cornstarch

⅛ cup water

Chengdu Chicken is named after Chengdu, the capital city of Szechuan province in western China.

1. Rinse the chicken breasts and cut into cubes. Cut the celery into 1-inch slices on the diagonal. Blanch or parboil the celery in a pot of boiling water for 2–3 minutes.
2. Combine the rice vinegar, sugar, ½ teaspoon salt, hot water, and rice wine. Set aside.
3. Add 1 tablespoon oil to a preheated wok or skillet. When the oil is hot, add the celery. Stir-fry briefly and add ¼ teaspoon salt. Stir-fry until the celery changes color and is tender but still firm. Remove from the wok.
4. Wipe the wok clean with a paper towel. Add ½ tablespoon oil. When the oil is hot, add the ginger and garlic and stir-fry briefly until aromatic. Add the chicken cubes. Stir-fry for 2–3 minutes, then add the hot bean sauce. Stir-fry until the chicken changes color and is nearly cooked through.
5. Add the sauce and bring to a boil. Mix the cornstarch and water and add to the middle of the wok, stirring vigorously to thicken. Add the celery. Mix everything through and serve hot.

Chicken Lettuce Wraps

 Yields 5 wraps

$ Total Cost: $4.40

½ pound boneless, skinless chicken breasts

½ head lettuce leaves

½ red bell pepper

½ 4-ounce can water chestnuts, rinsed and drained

½ 4-ounce can bamboo shoots, rinsed and drained

½ tablespoon soy sauce

1 tablespoon oyster sauce

½ tablespoon Chinese rice wine or dry sherry

½ teaspoon sugar

2 tablespoons oil for stir-frying

½ teaspoon minced garlic clove

½ teaspoon minced ginger

½ stalk celery, thinly sliced on the diagonal

½ tablespoon cornstarch mixed with 2 tablespoons water

1 green onions, thinly sliced on the diagonal

½ teaspoon sesame oil

Crisp lettuce makes an interesting contrast to the warm chicken and vegetable filling. To keep the lettuce leaves crisp, chill until ready to use.

1. Wash the chicken and pat dry. Pound lightly on the chicken to tenderize. Cut the chicken into thin slices approximately 2½ inches long. Wash the lettuce, and dry and separate the leaves. Set aside. Remove the seeds from the red pepper and chop into bite-sized pieces. Slice the water chestnuts and cut the bamboo shoots into 1-inch pieces.

2. Mix together the soy sauce, oyster sauce, Chinese rice wine, and sugar. Set aside.

3. Add 2 tablespoons oil in a preheated wok or heavy skillet. When oil is hot, add the garlic and ginger. Stir-fry briefly until aromatic. Add the chicken and stir-fry until it is browned and nearly cooked through. Remove from the wok and set aside. Drain on paper towels.

4. Add 2 tablespoons oil. When oil is hot, add the water chestnuts and celery. Stir-fry for about 1 minute, then add the red pepper. Add the bamboo shoots. Stir-fry until the vegetables are brightly colored and tender. Add the sauce. Give the cornstarch/water mixture a quick stir and add in the middle, stirring quickly to thicken. Stir in the green onions. Drizzle with sesame oil.

5. To prepare the lettuce wraps, lay a lettuce leaf flat. Place one-fifth of the chicken combined with the vegetable/sauce mixture into the middle and roll up the lettuce leaf. Continue with the remainder of the chicken and lettuce leaves. Serve as an appetizer, or as a main course with stir-fried rice vermicelli.

Savory Shanghai Noodles

Serves 2–4

Total Cost: $4.79

½ pound boneless, skinless chicken breasts (cubed)

½ teaspoon sugar

½ teaspoon cornstarch

½ bunch spinach

¾ cup chicken broth

¼ cup water

1 tablespoon plus 2 teaspoons oyster sauce

1 teaspoon Chinese rice wine or dry sherry

1 garlic clove, finely chopped

1 slice ginger, finely chopped

½ pound fresh Shanghai noodles

½ teaspoon sesame oil

1¼ cups oil for frying

Noodle Lore

Contrary to popular legend, the Italians were probably twirling linguine and spaghetti noodles on their plates long before Marco Polo made his famous trek to China and the Far East. However, it is true that the Chinese have been enjoying noodles since ancient times. Symbolizing a long life in Chinese culture, noodles occupy an important place in festive celebrations such as Chinese New Year. And birthday celebrations wouldn't be complete without a heaping bowl of longevity noodles.

Frying the chicken briefly in 1 cup of hot oil gives it a soft, velvety texture.

1. Rinse the chicken in warm water and pat dry. Marinate the chicken in the sugar and cornstarch for 15 minutes.
2. Wash the spinach and drain thoroughly. Mix together the chicken broth, water, oyster sauce, and rice wine, and set aside.
3. Add 1¼ cups oil to a preheated wok or skillet. When oil is hot, add the chicken and fry briefly for 1 minute. Remove the chicken from the wok with a slotted spoon and drain on paper towels.
4. Remove all but 2 tablespoons oil from the wok. Add the spinach and fry until it changes color. Add seasonings such as salt or soy sauce, if desired. Remove from the wok and set aside.
5. Add the garlic and ginger and stir-fry briefly until aromatic. Add the noodles. Stir-fry and toss with the sesame oil. Make a well in the middle of the wok and add the sauce. Bring to a boil. Add the spinach and the chicken back into the wok. Mix everything through and serve hot.

CHAPTER 15

VEGETABLE DISHES

Stir-Fried Bok Choy

Serves 2–4

1 bok choy

2 tablespoons oil for stir-frying

¼ teaspoon salt

1½ tablespoons water

Serve on the side, or use to enliven a basic meat dish such as Basic Chicken Stir-Fry (Chapter 14).

1. Separate each stalk and leaves. Cut the stalks diagonally into 1-inch pieces. Cut the leaves crosswise into 1-inch pieces.
2. Add the oil to a preheated wok or skillet. When oil is hot, add the bok choy stalks. Stir-fry for about 1 minute and then add the leaves. Add salt, sprinkle the water over, and cover and cook on medium heat, until the bok choy is tender but still firm and not mushy.

Three Vegetable Stir-Fry

Serves 2

2 ounces snow peas

¾ tablespoons oil for stir-frying

½ can baby corn, rinsed and drained

3 shiitake mushrooms, sliced

½ tablespoon dark soy sauce

¼ teaspoon sugar

¼ teaspoon salt

The combination of shiitake mushrooms, snow peas, and baby corn provides an interesting contrast in color and texture. Serve with a more highly seasoned dish.

1. Wash and string the snow peas.
2. Add oil to a preheated wok or frying pan. Add the baby corn and stir-fry briefly, then add the snow peas. Stir-fry until the snow peas turn a bright green. Push them up to the side and add the mushrooms. Add the dark soy sauce, sugar, and salt. Mix through.

Stir-Fried Water Chestnuts and Bamboo Shoots

 Serves 2

 Total Cost: $1.58

1 tablespoon oil for stir-frying

½ teaspoon minced ginger

1 4-ounce can bamboo shoots, rinsed and drained

⅛ teaspoon salt

½ can water chestnuts, rinsed and drained

¼ cup chicken broth

½ tablespoon soy sauce

½ teaspoon sugar

½ green onion, cut into 1½-inch pieces

Use this basic recipe anytime you want to stir-fry vegetables. The only thing that will change is the stir-frying time for different types of vegetables.

1. Cut the water chestnuts in half.
2. Add the oil to a preheated wok or skillet. When the oil is hot, add the ginger. Stir-fry briefly until aromatic. Add the bamboo shoots. Stir-fry for 1–2 minutes, and add the salt. Mix in and add the water chestnuts. Stir-fry for 1–2 more minutes, and then add the chicken broth, soy sauce, and sugar.
3. Bring the broth to a boil, and then turn down the heat and simmer for a few more minutes, until everything is nicely cooked through. Stir in the green onion and serve.

Stir-Frying in Order

Stir-fry vegetables according to density, adding the thickest vegetables to the wok first, so that they cook longest. If you're uncertain about the correct order, just stir-fry all the vegetables separately and add back into the wok during the final stages of cooking.

The $5 Takeout Cookbook

Vegetable Chop Suey

Serves 2

¼ cup water chestnuts, fresh or canned

½ green bell pepper

½ red bell pepper

½ bunch bok choy

¼ pound snow peas

2 tablespoons oil for stir-frying

⅛ teaspoon salt

¾ tablespoons water

¼ teaspoon minced ginger

¼ teaspoon minced garlic

¼ red onion, chopped

½ cup fresh mushrooms

½ teaspoon sugar

½ carrot, thinly sliced on the diagonal

¼ cup mung bean sprouts, rinsed and drained

½ tablespoon cornstarch

2 tablespoons water

1 tablespoon oyster sauce

Don't have any bok choy on hand? You can use broccoli instead of bok choy and green beans instead of snow peas.

1. Clean the mushrooms with a damp towel and slice. If using fresh water chestnuts, wash and peel. If using canned, rinse in warm water and slice. Cut the green and red bell peppers in half, remove the seeds, and cut into thin strips. For the bok choy, separate each stalk and leaves. Cut the stalk diagonally and cut the leaves across. Wash and string the snow peas. Add 1 table-spoon oil to a preheated wok or frying pan. When oil is ready, add the bok choy stalks. Cook for about 1 minute, then add the leaves. Add the salt, and sprinkle with water. Cover and cook on medium heat until the bok choy is tender but still firm. Remove and set aside.

2. Wipe out the wok with a paper towel and add 1 tablespoon of oil. When oil is ready, add the ginger and garlic and stir-fry until aromatic. Add the red onion and stir-fry. Remove from the wok and set aside. Add the green and red peppers and the snow peas. Stir-fry for about a minute, then add the mushrooms and ½ teaspoon of sugar and continue stir-frying. Remove from the wok and set aside. Add the water chestnuts and carrot. Stir-fry for a minute, then add the bean sprouts.

3. Mix cornstarch and water, then stir in the oyster sauce. Add the removed vegetables back into the wok and mix. Make a well in the center and gradually add the cornstarch/oyster sauce mixture, stirring to thicken. Bring to a boil, remove from the heat, and serve hot.

Spicy Eggplant Stir-Fry

 Serves 2

½ eggplant

1½ tablespoon oil for
  stir-frying

1 tablespoon red rice vinegar

¼ teaspoon brown sugar

1 tablespoon soy sauce

½ tablespoon chopped garlic

¼ teaspoon chili paste

⅛ teaspoon sesame oil

This dish can be made with truncheon-shaped Chinese eggplant or the thicker eggplant commonly available in local supermarkets.

1. Wash the eggplant, cut off the ends, and slice diagonally into 1-inch pieces.
2. Add oil to a preheated wok or skillet. When the oil is hot, add the eggplant slices, stir-frying in batches if necessary. Stir-fry for about 2–3 minutes.
3. Add the red rice vinegar, brown sugar, soy sauce, garlic, and chili paste, and mix through. Drizzle the sesame oil over and give a final stir.

Braised Baby Bok Choy

 Serves 2

2 bunches baby bok choy

¼ cup chicken stock or broth

¼ cup water

½ teaspoon sugar

¾ teaspoon rice vinegar

1 tablespoon oil for stir-frying

1 garlic clove, finely chopped

¼ teaspoon sesame oil

Also called Shanghai bok choy, baby bok choy has a sweeter flavor and is more tender than regular bok choy.

1. Wash and drain the baby bok choy. Cut off the roots and separate the stalks and leaves.
2. Combine the chicken stock, water, sugar, and rice vinegar.
3. Add oil to a preheated wok or skillet. When oil is ready, add the garlic. Stir-fry until aromatic.
4. Add the bok choy stalks and stir-fry until they turn a bright green. While stir-frying the stalks, add the leaves.
5. Add the chicken broth mixture. Turn down the heat and simmer, covered, for 5 minutes. Turn off the heat and drizzle with the sesame oil.

Better Bok Choy

For best results, always separate bok choy stalks from the leaves prior to stir-frying, as the thick stalks take longer to cook. At the other end, be careful not to overcook the bok choy.

Index

Note: Page numbers in **bold** indicate recipe category lists.

ABOUT THE AUTHORS

Rhonda Lauret Parkinson (Calgary, Alberta, Canada) is the author of *The Everything®* *Chinese Cookbook* and *The Everything® Fondue Cookbook*. She is a freelance writer and chef.

Margaret Kaeter (St. Paul, MN) is the author of *The Everything® Mexican Cookbook* and *The Everything® Holiday Cookbook*. Her extensive articles on health and nutrition have appeared in publications such as *New Woman*, *BEEF*, and *Entrepreneur*.

Belinda Hulin (Atlantic Beach, FL) is the author of *The Everything® Pizza Cookbook* and *The Everything® Fondue Party Book*. She served as food editor of the *Florida Times-Union* for five years and is a recipient of several Association of Food Journalist awards.

Jennifer Malott Kotylo (Chicago, IL) is the author of *The Everything® Thai Cookbook*. She is a freelance writer, editor, and marketing consultant, who has served as the treasurer of the Chicago Chapter of the American Institute of Wine & Food.